Proclaiming God's Truth

The First 25 Years at Christian Light Publications 1969 - 1994

By

John Coblentz, Merna Shank, and others

Christian Light Publications, Inc.

Harrisonburg, Virginia 22801

ISBN: 0-87813-558-8
Printed in U.S.A.

Introduction

F or whatsoever things were written aforetime were written for our learning, that we through patience and comfort of the Scriptures might have hope" (Romans 15:4).

This verse gives us Biblical purpose for chronicling the events of God's people for God's people. Much of the Bible is the record of history—what God's people did and did not do, what needs and problems and difficulties they went through, how they called upon God, and how God answered.

The people at CLP, like the people in Bible stories, are ordinary people, subject to limitations, prone at times to failure, but eternally grateful to the God who is patient enough to work with human beings and powerful enough to turn their feeble efforts into eternal good.

As a publishing company, CLP contributes a very small drop to the mighty bucket of ink that pours into printing presses today. Furthermore, this history covers only twenty-five quick years—a brief millisecond in time. Why this story then? Because this history is HIS story. And as the psalmist cried, "He hath made his wonderful works to be remembered" (Psalm 111:4a). This is a tribute to the One and only One who is worthy of praise. "By him therefore let us offer the sacrifice of praise to God continually, that is, the fruit of our lips giving thanks to his name" (Hebrews 13:15).

Contents

INTRODUCTION   iii

TIME LINE OF CLP   vi

PART I: THE FOUNDING OF CLP   1969-1971   1
Park View Press   1
Incorporation of Christian Light Publications   2
Tax Exempt Status   4
Emerging Identity   6
CLP and the Association of Mennonite Elementary
Schools   8
First Publications   9

PART II: THE EXPANDING YEARS   1972-1978   13
Sunday School Curriculum   13
Writers and Artists' Conference   21
Bible School Curriculum   24
Just for You   28
Arrive Alive   34
Social Studies Series   36

PART III: CHRISTIAN LIGHT EDUCATION   1979-   43
Negotiations With ACE   45
Alpha Omega Publications   47
Production of CLE Curriculum   48
The First School Year   52
Star Revision   53
The Quality of CLE   54
How Was CLE Funded?   59
CLE and Park View Press   64
CLE Homestudy Growth   65
The Extension Committee   69

CLE Teacher Training   74
CLE Workshops   76
PART IV: THE SHADOW OF DEATH   1988-1991   79
Cancer   79
Final Days   81
Another Death   83
They Died in Faith   83
PART V: CLP EMPLOYEES   85
Dedication   85
Voluntary Service   92
Keeping in Touch   95
Employees at Work   98
Current Committees   112
Testimonies From CLP Board Members   116
PART VI: CLP TODAY   121
Reorganization   121
Special Publications   122
Original Curriculum   127
Improved Facilities   130
FROM WRITER TO READER   149
OUR DAILY PRAYER (song)   156
APPENDIX A: CLP Employees   157
APPENDIX B: Directors / Advisors / Editors   169
APPENDIX C: CLP Publications   172

Time Line of CLP

1969— Incorporation of Christian Light Publications

1970— First public business; beginning of *Just for You*

1971— First book published: *Allegheny Gospel Trails*

1972— Beginning of Sunday school materials

1973— First issue of *Companions*; first Writers' Conference

1974— First social studies textbook published: *Living Together on God's Earth*

1975— Began writing Bible school curriculum

1976— Second social studies textbook: *God's World, His Story*

1977— Hard at work on Bible school curriculum

1978— Bible school curriculum available

1979— Contract with AOP to develop Christian Light Education materials

1980— First year CLE available for schools (100 schools and home schools)

1981— Busy producing CLE curriculum

1982— CLP began doing its own printing, sharing equipment with PVP

1983— A year of difficulties and tests in different areas, but surrounded by God's faithfulness and blessings

1984— Beginning of Star Revision of CLE

1985— First extensive efforts to provide CLE exhibits for homeschool conventions

1986— Moved Writers' Conference to a larger location

1987— First issue of *Alight*

1988— Extension Committee formed to handle requests for spiritual help and fellowship; purchase of PVP's printing equipment

1989— Busy with details of new construction planning; first steps taken toward development of Spanish school curriculum

1990— Death of Sanford Shank, Founder and Director of CLP

1991— Reorganization of CLP; death of Sterling Shank

1992— Moved into Building No. 2

1993— Tenth printing of *Arrive Alive*, total over 1,000,000 copies printed

1994— 32,000 people using Christian Light Sunday school materials

Over 500 schools using CLE materials

Over 4,000 homeschools using CLE materials

Part I: The Founding of CLP, 1969-1971

LORD, thou hast been our dwellingplace in all generations. Before the mountains were brought forth, or ever thou hadst formed the earth and the world, even from everlasting to everlasting, thou art God (Psalm 90:1, 2).

The story of Christian Light Publications actually begins more than twenty-five years ago. As a teenager who was not a great reader, Sanford Shank sensed the need for more wholesome literature for conservative people. As a college student who was not an exceptional scholar, he sensed the need for godly curriculum material. As a young man who had grown up in the country, he relinquished the security of his father's farm and became a self-employed printer, even though he knew next-to-nothing about printing.

Park View Press

Park View Press was the business resulting from that venture into the lithographic printing process based on the simple principle that oil and water do not mix. For Sanford it was an untried field in 1957. He might easily have become discouraged if he had known how much there was to learn besides his initial instructions in producing good copy with a small offset press. He would also have been surprised that thirty reams of 8 1/2 x 11 paper was a very small order, and that fifteen years later, paper in 400-pound rolls would be delivered by the truckload.

Although farm experience may have seemed like unsuitable

1

preparation for printing, Sanford marveled many times at the way his boyhood experience equipped him to work with complicated printing machinery. Still it was not easy. What the work demanded that he did not understand, he learned through personal study, assistance from business suppliers, long hours on the job, and perseverance through trial and error.

Original Park View Press Building built in 1960. A second floor was added over this part in 1970.

Incorporation of Christian Light Publications

If Sanford knew next-to-nothing about printing, he knew even less about publishing. Having a shop with typesetting, printing, and bindery equipment and knowing how to operate it was not enough. Simply printing what other people want published is not the same as developing, producing, and marketing one's own materials. Furthermore, the operation of a successful printing business could be very time consuming, leaving little time for pursuing the vision of publishing Christian literature.

But Sanford could not escape the strong sense that the Lord would be honored with solidly Biblical materials. If it was the Lord's will to have such materials, would He not also enable His people to produce them?

Because he had a printing facility, other people began to share their concern. New literature was needed for conservative Mennonite people. Every concerned person who spoke to Sanford

Sanford and Merna Shank worked together in planning and operating PVP. When Sanford's time became more involved in administrative responsibilities, Merna served as his secretary.

about this need found an ear ready to listen.

Sanford's wife, Merna, was a constant encouragement in the development of Sanford's vision. Prior to their marriage in 1956, she had taught business education and typing courses at a local high school. Her secretarial skills, editorial skills, and proofreading skills fit in well with her husband's vision for publishing.

The first concrete steps toward publishing took place in August 1965. Enough people had talked to Sanford that he decided the time had come to present the matter to a broader audience. He called a meeting of bishops, ministers, teachers, and writers to discuss the needs and possibilities for Christian publishing.

Twelve church leaders, including several members of *The Sword and Trumpet* staff, participated in that first meeting. Between August and November, three meetings were held. The general consensus was that material was needed, especially for Sunday school, but rather than form a new organization, the venture should proceed under the publishers of *The Sword and Trumpet*.

The Sword and Trumpet Board was enlarged, and by the end of 1966 a limited amount of Sunday school material was being published. Park View Press did the printing. Sword and Trumpet also selected devotional books and Bible study helps from other publishers and offered them for sale through their magazine—a quarterly publication that became a monthly at the beginning of 1967.

Although this met some needs, many possible publications such as devotional and doctrinal books, school textbooks, and tracts remained untouched. Members of the Sword and Trumpet Board were sympathetic to the idea of producing these materials, but they did not feel they could take on the responsibility of publication. The need still remained for a full literature ministry, a consistent voice for evangelism and nurture.

Ray Shenk, member of the first Board of Directors. He served as a Director from 1969 to 1982 and Director Emeritus until his death in 1985.

About this time Ray Shenk, a minister from Maryland, spoke to Sanford, indicating that through the sale of property he would be interested in making a sizable donation to the publication of sound literature. After considerable thought, prayer, and discussion, Christian Light Publications was incorporated as a non-profit organization in June, 1969. The first Board of Directors included Ray Shenk and Sanford and Merna Shank. As the work progressed, more members were added. Today, a six-member board directs CLP operations.

According to the charter of incorporation, CLP's purpose was, "To disseminate Christian information and to engage in activities for the promotion of the Christian ethic and Christian living." In more down-to-earth terms the Board was wanting to provide literature and educational materials that presented God's Word as the source of truth, that applied the doctrines of Christ practically, that attracted sinners to salvation through Christ, and that spiritually nurtured believers. Above all, of course, the purpose was to glorify the Lord.

Tax Exempt Status

Founding CLP was easier than carrying it forward. There were plans and visions, but concrete, realistic projections were difficult.

These projections were necessary in written form, however, for the Internal Revenue Service to grant CLP tax exemption status. And so, projections were hammered out. After various exchanges of communication and delays, tax exemption was finally granted on July 14, 1970. CLP was recognized as a nonprofit public foundation, and people could count their donations as tax deductible gifts.

Being a small publishing company, CLP's tax exempt status was especially needful. Publishing ventures are expensive. Finished products, published on a small scale of several thousand copies, seldom can be sold at a price that recovers all the cost of development, production, storage, and distribution. From a financial standpoint, much of the material CLP has produced has been indeed nonprofit. Donations have carried this work along, and besides, have made it possible to offer many tracts and other evangelistic literature free of charge.

(Nonprofit status, of course, does not mean that a business cannot operate profitably, or that its employees may not earn a living. Nonprofit means that no individual can personally profit from the earnings or receipts of the organization, and should the business ever dissolve, funds received from the sale of assets may go only to another nonprofit organization.)

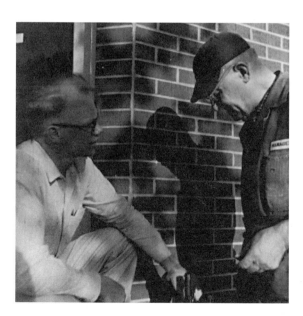

Sanford Shank and Aldine Brenneman discussing some aspect of maintenance or repair.

Emerging Identity

Because Christian Light Publications was born out of a close working relationship between Park View Press and Sword and Trumpet, a number of years elapsed until CLP emerged with its own identity. The similarities of the organizations and the close proximity of their work caused understandable questions for onlookers: What is the difference between Christian Light Publications and Park View Press? What is the difference between CLP and Sword and Trumpet?

Some did not understand the distinction between printing and publishing. Park View Press was Sanford Shank's personal printing business. Both Christian Light Publications and Sword and Trumpet were publishing operations whose printing was done by Park View Press.

Two men on the CLP Board also served on the Sword and Trumpet Board (although neither was on one as a result of the other). Furthermore, both CLP and Sword and Trumpet had their business offices on Park View Press's premises. Neither Sword and Trumpet nor Christian Light Publications had sufficient need to justify hiring full-time office help. In a cooperative

arrangement with Park View Press, however, PVP employees were loaned to either publisher as needed. This continued even after CLP established its own payroll in 1971. Once a month, accounts were settled between the organizations—each paying the other for work done for them by employees on the other's payroll.

To help clarify some of the confusion, CLP issued a pamphlet for general distribution entitled "What Is Christian Light Publications?" In addition, they issued a page and a half explanation for their employees: "So Many People Are Confused!" Even one CLP Board member acknowledged that he came to a full understanding for the first time only after reading these papers.

Although this system was confusing to onlookers, it was not as complicated as it could be made to sound. For instance, an outsider asked one employee who she was working for. She replied, "CLP." She went on to say, however, that she was working on a bindery job for Park View Press, who was doing it for Campbell Copy Center, who was printing it for Rod and Staff. If an outsider had difficulty understanding such a mixture, at least the point was made that printers and publishers can cooperate!

Another distinction necessary for some people was the relationship of Christian Light Publications to Southeastern Mennonite Conference. All of CLP's local Board members have been members of Southeastern Conference, giving the impression to some that CLP was a Conference organization.

CLP did not originate as a Southeastern Conference venture, however, and remained independent of any one conference or group for reasons outlined in the "Statement of Understanding" for Board members and advisors. Part of that statement reads as follows:

> This organization has no members; all of its affairs are regulated and directed by the Board of Directors, which is a self-perpetuating body. . . .
>
> Since CLP was established in response to the call of the Lord to provide Christian nurture and evangelism literature for a Mennonite constituency, and since many leaders, groups, and individuals from this constituency have appealed to CLP to supply literature for their use, and since this constituency is made up of many congregations, conferences, and fellowships which function as totally independent organizations, we as the CLP Board of Directors reaffirm our dedication to the production of material that is Scripturally sound and supports Scriptural application of Biblical principles made by a given church body.
>
> This means that we endeavor to cultivate loyalty to the local church in Scriptural application of Biblical principles.
>
> Therefore, we refrain from organizational control by any of the constituent groups, recognizing that such involvement would tend to limit the applications to those of the controlling church body, or on the other hand, could

deteriorate into carelessness in teaching Scriptural principles if different church bodies would share in control.

We do, however, feel the need for contact with representative personnel from various parts of the country and church; therefore, we have invited individuals from various areas to accept the Board of Directors' appointment to serve as Advisors to it. The Directors ask these persons to share with us their counsel. In turn they share with Advisors information about development, needs, and proposals, asking them to respond to us and share with others as they have opportunities and would like to do so.

At present eleven advisors from eight states and provinces serve on the Advisory Board.

CLP and the Association of Mennonite Elementary Schools

A number of years before CLP was formed, Sanford Shank had numerous brainstorming sessions with Sanford Shetler and Clarence Fretz (both of whom were educators) about the needs and possibilities for a Christian school curriculum. As a follow-up of one discussion, Sanford Shetler produced an outline for a social studies series. At that time, however, such a project did not seem possible without an organization to guide and support it.

John Hartzler, before becoming CLP's Business Manager in 1975 and General Manager in 1979, worked in the pressroom and bindery for more than 4 years.

Boyd Shank, who gave Sanford his first training in practical mechanics on the farm, was able to successfully transfer his own skills to the pressroom where he worked for many years.

With the formation of Christian Light Publications, however, the outlook was brighter. Brother Fretz immediately began to explore the possibility of CLP working with the Association of Mennonite Elementary Schools (AMES). Beginning in January of 1970, CLP handled much of AMES's business, including stocking their materials, filling orders, keeping their mailing list current, and sending out their periodical, *The Christian School*. This was a welcome relief to the organizers of AMES, since before this all their work had been done by volunteer teachers and educators whose schedules were already taxed.

Although CLP's relationship with AMES did not result in the production of school materials directly, it proved to be a blessing by introducing CLP to the educational market. When AMES disbanded in 1975, CLP purchased the publishing rights for two workbooks (written by Clarence Fretz) which AMES had produced previously—*Story of God's People* and *You and Your Bible/You and Your Life*. CLP has continued to produce these workbooks.

First Publications

About four months into 1970, CLP produced its first publication—*Just for You*, a monthly paper designed to meet a variety of needs for the saved and the unsaved. The growth of this little publishing venture has been so exceptional that a separate section will be devoted to telling the story. A step of faith was needed to print the 3,000 copies of the first issue. Today, more than 80,000 copies are printed each month. Donations have made it possible to offer this evangelizing/nurturing message free of charge month after month, even though some orders have been as large as 800,000 copies (for a variety of issues).

CLP published its first book in 1971. *Allegheny Gospel Trails* by Virginia Crider told the story of Rhine and Anna Benner's missionary work in West Virginia in the early 1900s. With the 5,000-copy printing of this book, CLP officially became a publisher of Christian biography.

Also in 1971, CLP published its first commentary. Sanford Shetler wrote a commentary on I Corinthians entitled *Paul's Letter to the Corinthians, 55 A.D.* At that time the plan was for this book to be the first in a "Compact Commentary Series." Although quite a few copies of Shetler's work have been sold in hardcover and paperback editions, no more commentaries have been produced in this series.

The year 1971 was a milestone in a number of other ways. During

Aldine Brenneman (Merna Shank's father), who served at CLP in various ways from its beginning until 1985.

this year Christian Light Publications established its own payroll and began hiring full-time employees. Lloyd Hartzler, who still serves as office editor, was the first employee to be hired. Three months later, John Martin came on staff as a writer and editor. He was the first and only employee who worked at CLP in an assignment approved by the Selective Service Board as an alternative to military service. The discontinuation of the draft likely was the reason there were no more requests for alternative service assignments.

In addition to writing the monthly *Just for You*, John Martin also embarked in 1971 on another "first" for CLP—a social studies textbook. In the years previous, whenever the need for school curriculum had been discussed, Christian social studies textbooks had emerged as the most urgent need. The cost of such a venture, however, seemed overwhelming. There was not only the research and writing to do, but mapwork and full-color photos were to be included. But by 1974 the third grade textbook, *Living Together on God's Earth,* was completed and ready for use.

From an Employee

The September after my graduation from high school, I began my four years of higher education. Not at a local college, but at Park View Press.

The first year I got my theological education working between Lloyd Hartzler and John Martin..

The first year was also the most distinct. The other three that I spent working in my corner downstairs are sort of blended into one. Not that I spent all my time in the corner. Far from it. I was glad for the spice that a variety of jobs gave to my working hours.

I learned many things. . . . such as the fact that one can't always rely on first impressions or even second, third, and fourth impressions.

I learned that constructive criticism is a part of certain jobs. . . .

I learned that where there are Christians, it is possible to have harmony, even though the people and some of their views are very different.

So I want to thank each one of you for your part in my education and your kindness to me. . . .

I shall always remember with pleasure my four years of higher education. —Hilda (Swartz) Barnhart

Part II: The Expanding Years, 1972-1978

Except the LORD build the house, they labour in vain that build it: except the LORD keep the city, the watchman waketh but in vain (Psalm 127:1).

Sunday School Curriculum

In 1972 the Sword and Trumpet Board approached CLP about the possibility of taking over the publication of Sunday school materials, which Sword and Trumpet had begun more than five years before. CLP was only three years old, and the prospect of supplying Sunday school materials to churches across the nation seemed like an overwhelming task. More writers, artists, editors, committees, and finances would be needed.

In a special session on September 17, 1972, the CLP Board discussed the implications of accepting this offer. After considerable discussion, the consensus of the Board was to explore with Sword and Trumpet the terms of transfer. Both boards wanted to see the change made as smoothly as possible for the sake of those already using the Sunday school curriculum, and so, through numerous meetings they worked out an agreement.

Consequently an announcement signed by the chairman of both boards was sent to the joint constituencies. A part of that announcement follows:

The Sword and Trumpet Magazine was launched in 1929 by the late Bishop George R. Brunk as a publication devoted to the defense of Biblical faith. The magazine has published

13

continuously since that time with the exception of a few years after George R. Brunk's death.

In 1943 Sword and Trumpet was reorganized under a board of interested brethren serving voluntarily, and since that time has gradually expanded its interest in the production and promotion of sound Christian literature. In 1967 the publication of Sunday school materials was added to the work of this board.

Subsequently, a group of brethren within and without The Sword and Trumpet board became interested in the production of Christian literature in a larger way than had been envisioned in The Sword and Trumpet organization. In 1969 these brethren formed another organization incorporated as Christian Light Publications.

The interests of these two organizations have run in parallel and overlapping paths so that some division of responsibilities and interests seemed advisable.

Accordingly, the boards of these two organizations have agreed by proper negotiation and action of both boards, that as of December 1, 1972, the Christian Light Publications board will assume responsibility for the publication of Sunday school materials and related Christian literature

Mylinda (Howard) Turner (foreground) and Ann Custer using the Mergenthaler keyboards which prepared tapes that were run through a printer to obtain final layout copy. Note the rolls of perforated tapes hanging on the pegboard ready for the printer.

Mark Heatwole, now a Board member, worked as an employee from 1978-84. Here he is operating the continuous feed folder.

while The Sword and Trumpet board will continue responsibility for publication of the magazine.

The brethren who make up the boards of these two organizations are pledged to continue working in the common purpose of producing and disseminating Christian literature. Both The Sword and Trumpet magazine and the Sunday school materials (which will now be published by Christian Light Publications) will continue under the same philosophy and objectives.

Production of Sunday school materials has expanded considerably since the beginning years. Six Sunday school quarterlies, plus teachers' guides, and three weekly take-home papers are produced regularly to meet the needs of preschoolers through adults. On any given Sunday, if it were possible to see them, you could find approximately 32,000 people in more

than 500 locations using CLP Sunday school literature.
The Sunday school materials are used in several countries besides the United States and Canada, and although many users are Mennonites, not all are. A man in the Midwest wrote that other Christian businessmen in his area and he were conducting Sunday school classes at the Veterans Administration Center Chapel. He was 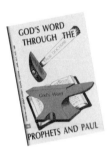 using CLP materials when he taught. As the other men gradually discontinued their teaching for lack of interest, his class was growing, and he was teaching nearly every Sunday. Reflecting on the interest of his students, he wrote, "They and I appreciate sound literature."

Another man told about the change he observed in his youth class when he began using CLP material. His pupils, who had been having trouble "getting hold" of the Sunday school lessons, began to enjoy them, and six of them gave their hearts to the Lord.

Sunday school quarterlies are being used other than in Sunday school. One non-Mennonite mother wrote for samples of CLP materials after her son had used them in his Bible class at the

Sanford Shank operating the Heidelberg Press. At some time during the history of Park View Press and Christian Light Publications, Sanford worked at all the operations and machines required by the business.

16

Christian school he attended. Another mother said she used them for Bible lessons with her five-year-old in her homeschool kindergarten program. One user asked for several teachers' guides to be used in teaching a children's group on Sunday evening. Many quarterlies are recycled and sent to various foreign countries. For example, one user gathers his church's used Sunday school materials and sends them to workers in a youth camp in a large city in Africa where they gladly use all he can send.

In 1982 CLP issued a special quarterly study on the doctrine of nonresistance. It was followed in 1986 with a quarter's study on the doctrine of nonconformity. These undated studies, entitled *Nonresistance—God's Plan for the Church* and *Separation and Nonconformity,* are still carried in inventory and continue to be used for midweek Bible studies and Bible school classes.

A number of years after the nonresistance quarterly was first used, CLP received a letter from a man of a non-Mennonite denomination who ordered copies for use among his own people. He wrote:

> Several years ago I attended a Mennonite church, and I really appreciated this Sunday school quarterly. It helped me find out where I stand and created a true conviction that I had never believed before. That of nonparticipation in war. Our church is mixed up about its peace stance and needs the aid of a Biblical study.

The three weekly take-home papers include *Story Mates* for preschoolers and primaries, *Partners* for juniors and intermediates, and *Companions* for youth and adults. Combined, these papers have a circulation of more than 18,500. The blessing they have brought to readers is one that only the Lord could have provided. One reader sent this challenge: "I am depending on your paper to help get my friends converted. They do not want me to talk to them about Jesus."

17

The work that goes into producing the story papers each week is eloquently reflected in the following two editorials from *Companions*. The first article was written by David Burkholder, who served for nine years as editor of the youth-adult paper.

The Challenge of Change

Someone has said, "There is nothing permanent except change." That is another way of saying that life is simply made up of a series of changes, and adjustments to changes. Only God does not change. The human experience is fraught with change. It is a continual part of our lives. We adjust, and move on.

And now change is coming to *Companions*. After more than nine years I am stepping aside as editor. My responsibilities end with this issue, January, 1983.

This has not been a hasty, nor easy decision. I have been struggling with the pressures of increasing responsibilities for some time now.

I am happy that Brother Roger Berry has accepted the task and will be assuming full editorship with the February issue. Roger is not a newcomer to *Companions*, having been editor of the "Truth for Youth" page.

I leave *Companions* with mingled feelings. I have enjoyed the work and feel God has blessed me in it. I trust you have been blessed, too, by the challenges and inspiration for Christian living from these pages.

Much effort goes into providing quality Christian reading material. I have read thousands of manuscripts and written nearly 100,000 words. It takes time and effort, but it is a worthwhile and worthy work. The printed page carries tremendous potential for Christian influence. I am glad I have been privileged to be a part of this effort these past years.

I have appreciated your prayers and words of encouragement and counsel. They have helped make the task easier.

I have deeply appreciated the work and cooperation of contributing editors, Roger Berry, Paul Reed, and John Risser. The office editorial staff has been most kind and patient in their help and counsel. I have also appreciated the cooperation of the production personnel. Everyone has helped make the work go smoothly.

Companions has been a team effort. I am happy to have been a part of the team these past nine years. It has been a growing and rewarding experience for me.

And now as I step aside, I ask that you continue your prayers for the ongoing effort. Pray for Roger. Encourage him, and the total staff.

May God bless you—and all of us—for His glory. Amen
—David

The second article presents Roger Berry's reflections in taking over as editor of *Companions*.

To Be or Not to Be—An Editor

That was the decision I faced about a month ago when Brother David Burkholder asked to be relieved of editorial duties. Perhaps if I had known all the work that Brother Dave did as editor of *Companions*, I would have thought thrice.

Now the job has been turned over to me lock, stock, and file drawers full. Now I *really do* appreciate all your labors, Dave!

Being an editor is one of those behind-the-scenes jobs that seldom earns laurel wreaths or public citations. Someone once commented to Dave, "What are editors for anyway? Can't people just send in their articles and get them printed?" Sounds simple, right?

Each contribution that comes must be read, evaluated, and duly recorded. Letters of acceptance and rejection must be sent. Accepted pieces must be edited; word lengths must be computed accurately. Sample sheets called dummies (no reflection on writers or editors) must be drawn up for each month's issue. Colors need to be chosen, typestyles picked, and the exact position of each article, story, and poem must be determined. If too few articles come in some month or if a short filler is needed, the editor may have to "beat the bushes" for more contributions or work up something himself.

After the typesetters have the material, the editor must follow it through. If it is typed and found too long, he must cut out precious lines. If it is too short, he must come up with more fillers.

Pray that the Lord will grant me wisdom for this task. Yes, the work often seems like just "busy work." More seriously, it is a spiritual responsibility. A new editor has a considerable responsibility to the spiritual groundwork that has been laid before. And Christian publications, like Christians themselves, need to grow in spirituality and usefulness.

The editor cannot do the work alone, of course. I am sure I will appreciate more than ever the Sunday school committee, other editors, and our faithful contributors.

Incidentally, Brother Dave has promised to remain in the ranks of *Companions* contributors. You will get to hear from him again! May God bless you, Dave, as you continue to write and to take up other responsibilities.

—RLB

Roger Berry, serving as general editor of Companions *since 1983, was editor of two regular columns in the paper from its beginning in 1973.*

Writers and Artists' Conference

The work of publishing quality Christian literature is demanding on many fronts. Although Christian Light Publications has recruited full-time writers, editors, and artists over the years, many manuscripts come from individuals writing in their homes, in their spare time, here a little, and there a little.

The desire to put on paper the convictions and inspirations of the heart is a worthy desire. The actual practice of writing, however, and

Treda Layman, part-time staff artist, and David Miller, preparing art.

the actual practice of illustrating and designing are demanding disciplines.

Part of Sanford Shank's vision was that conservative Mennonite people need to take up the challenge of articulating their faith with soundness and clarity. The church needs writers and artists, he believed, who can write and illustrate according to the standards of God's truth and who can do their work with excellence.

To encourage these skills, Christian Light Publications launched their first Writers and Artists' Conference in 1973. The goals of this conference were to stimulate interest in writing and illustrating among conservative people and to help them in practical, hands-on ways to hone their skills. The invitation in a recent year's program says it this way:

Do you have an interest in discovering, cultivating, or

refining your gifts in the areas of writing, art, or music? You are warmly invited to attend the Writers and Artists' Conference sponsored by Christian Light Publications. Lodging and meals, workshops and messages, all are provided on a freewill offering basis. . . .

The theme for this Writers and Artists' Conference is a reminder of Jesus' commission to us to teach all nations. Literature, be it article, illustration, poem, song, story, or lesson, is a key component in fulfilling this mandate. Though you may be occupied in some obscure corner, God can give your literary products wings to the ends of the earth. Pray that again this year we will be instructed, encouraged, and challenged with the need for laborers and the potential fruits of our labors.

The conference has been held annually since 1973. In the early years it was held on the premises of CLP and occasioned an annual clearing-away, cleaning-up flurry of activity to accommodate the 100-plus people who attended. As interest and attendance grew, CLP

The first Writers' Conference, held in 1973.

This annual conference was expanded to include artists by 1974 and has provided training, inspiration, and encouragement for approximately 100-150 writers and artists in each of the 22 sessions held thus far.

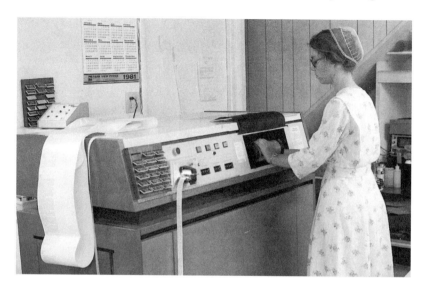

Sue (Heatwole) Anderson at the VIP typesetter which read the perforated tapes prepared at the keyboards. Copy produced by this machine on light sensitive paper needed to be processed in a dark room before it was ready to be used in layout copy. Different typestyles were available as small fonts on negatives which could be placed in the VIP.

moved the conference, first to the Pike Mennonite Church, then to the Berea Christian School, and most recently back to the renovated CLP headquarters.

The conference program typically has several inspirational messages for the entire group and numerous sectional workshops focused on a variety of skills, including article writing, Sunday school writing, short story writing, editing, art, poetry, and music composition.

Those who attend are encouraged to submit original work ahead of time for evaluation and helpful coaching. Many have testified to both the inspiration and practical discipline afforded by this annual conference. The following testimonies are illustrative:

"I really appreciate the conference and feel blessed to be able to attend."

"It was a blessing to be here again after missing two years. Of course, I always enjoy it."

"Probably the overall experience of interacting with others who have a vision (or burden) for writing was the most helpful. It has

Iva Trissel showing where film was loaded in the horizontal process camera used until 1992. This camera, which extended through the wall, opened into a darkroom where film was loaded.

intensified my conviction on writing as something needful, not just a hobby."

"I find the workshops invaluable. . . . I feel that the subjects of poetry, creative writing, short story writing, article writing, and art can never be worn out. I'd come every year just for the inspiration, even if the program were the same."

"I know planning and conducting this conference takes time and resources. However, since the inspiration and instruction are invaluable to us writers, please help us to continue writing and drawing by continuing these conferences. Thank you."

Bible School Curriculum

By 1974 people were frequently asking for CLP to consider producing a Bible school course. In a Board meeting in August of 1974, one man who served on the Advisory Board summed up his comments by saying, "I can see the handwriting on the wall. There ought to be more than thinking about this venture. There should be exploratory efforts put forth."

Accordingly, CLP appointed an Investigating Committee whose work included reviewing available curricula, contacting bookstores, and surveying CLP's constituency to determine interest in this project. In late 1974, the Board accepted the Investigating Committee's recommendation that under the Lord's leading, CLP should develop a new Bible school curriculum.

Following this decision, the Bible School Curriculum Committee appointed by the Board began the work of planning what the new curriculum should include. A "Through-the-Bible" study was eventually chosen. The Committee's work also included selecting writers, providing orientation and training sessions for the writers, arranging for the monumental amount of artwork needed for Bible school materials, and reviewing and editing the manuscripts in preparation for publication.

This project called for more personnel and more funds than even the Sunday school venture had. Accurate scheduling for writers, reviewers, and final editing was very difficult, but it soon became clear that the original projection to have half the curriculum ready by 1976 was not possible. Neither was it possible to have the entire work done by 1977. A firm goal was set for June 1, 1978.

Actual production began in the spring of 1977 and proceeded as manuscripts and art were available. By 1978, however, the production schedule was tight, and it seemed to tighten more and more as the finish date drew closer. Employees and volunteers from the church community worked long hours—some working during the day, and others filling in during evening and night shifts. The first item in the May 19 issue of *imPRESSions* (CLP employees' news sheet) read:

> We've made it! The last summer Bible school book came off the press at approximately 4 a.m. this morning. Cooperation between each one here has made it possible for us to accept our (over)work loads. Now we can all look forward to a breather as things settle back down to their normal hectic pace.

--- ***From an Employee*** ---

My work at Park View Press began about two months after the formation of Christian Light Publications. When PVP closed shop I was then officially employed by CLP, although I had worked on CLP jobs regularly almost from its beginning.

God really led in my coming to CLP. (In fact, it seemed He dragged me.) I needed a job, I prayed for a job, but I did not pay much heed to the word that PVP needed workers because I thought they wanted typists and I am *not* a typist.

My home was in Newport News, Va. The call came again

for workers and as Mother was planning to come up for a family reunion, I told her to investigate about a job for me. She called back, "I have a job for you and a place for you to stay." Two or three days later I was here.

As a child I loved coming to the valley to visit kinfolk and I loved the mountains. I thought we should move up here. Later, as my home church became more and more liberal, I longed for a more conservative fellowship. Both of these earlier prayers, as well as my need for a job, were answered when I came to PVP. Many times I have thanked God for His wonderful answers.

For the most part I have really enjoyed my work. I appreciate the Christian atmosphere, regular devotions together, the congenial working relationships, and the kind consideration of our supervisors in trying to suit the job and the hours to the needs of the employees. And it is wonderful being in God's work, helping to get out His Word, and trying to encourage others in serving Him.

—Betty Jane Brenneman

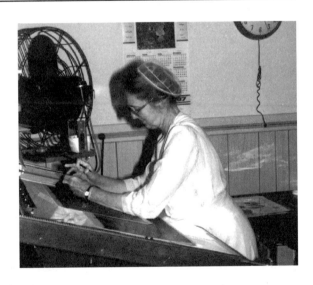

Betty Brenneman at work in the old stripping room located upstairs in Building No. 1.

The taxing work load did have its times of relaxation and irony. On one occasion, shortly before midnight the night shift decided to visit the ice cream stand a mile down the road. As CLP's general manager inserted his key into the front door on their return to work, he suddenly found himself the object of a police spotlight and inquiry. Upon being assured that the group did indeed have a reason and a right to enter the building at this unusual hour, the policeman returned to his nighttime patrol.

In recognition of the extra hard work, CLP closed the entire facility for one week of vacation that July, giving employees partial pay.

So it was that two preschool books and grades one through eight were available the summer of 1978. Grade one books, however, included cutout activities rather than the more convenient punch-outs available by the next printing. Grades nine and ten and an additional kindergarten book were added later. Recently, CLP prepared guidelines for teachers who need to use the curriculum in a five-day program.

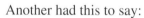

One user from Indiana wrote:

This summer I taught the fifth grade at our church's summer Bible school. I found our lessons in "God Corrects His People" to be interesting, informative, and very pertinent to us today. Both my students and I enthusiastically felt we learned much.

Another had this to say:

After having used CLP Bible school materials this summer I want to express my deep appreciation for the excellent work done in preparing these.

I had a very large class of 2nd graders. The Bible stories are put up so that my pupils would sit and eagerly listen for the whole story. One of the student's parents came to tell me that their son, who is not one to come home and tell them of what goes on, volunteered the story of baby Moses and did not miss one detail.

Besides its widespread use by churches in summer Bible school, this material is used in winter Bible schools and midweek classes. It is also used by Christian schools and homeschools.

A mother from West Virginia told how she used the Bible school materials in her home: "We have a family devotional period every evening, and I plan on using the 'Through-the-Bible' series to teach our little ones. I hope to purchase the whole series eventually so we can go through it grade by grade."

CLP sentiment is well expressed in the words of one Canadian brother who wrote, "I am trusting that some more souls will be in heaven instead of hell on account of daily vacation Bible school."

Just For You

In April of 1970, when the first issue of *Just for You* rolled off the press, no one knew where the Lord would take this evangelistic venture. As the original tract said, "*JUST FOR YOU* is designed to bring YOU 'a word in season' for varied experiences and personal needs."

As the Lord directed editors to improve the content and appearance of *Just for You* and gave increased vision to contributors and distributors, monthly printings climbed from 3,000 in 1970 to more than 80,000 in 1993.

Just for You is distributed in hundreds of places.

Since *Just for You*'s are intended to meet the needs of people wherever they are, that is where they are distributed—everywhere.

From an Employee

It has been good to be involved in the work of Christian Light Publications. I have worked at different jobs, but much of it has been in the mailing area which has included quite a lot of periodical mailing. I am glad to have a part in getting the Gospel message out through Christian literature. The *Just for You* tract has been one of my mailing jobs, and we mail many thousands each month.

I am glad the Lord led me to CLP. It has been a privilege to have a part in the work and to have Christian co-workers. May God bless our efforts to His glory and to the saving of many souls.   —Zela Shenk

---

Zela Shenk checking employee daily time sheets, one of her many jobs.

Incoming mail from an uncounted number of communities and countries has mentioned more than thirty kinds of places the papers have been given or received: in business offices, mail routes, airplanes, military bases, schools, service stations, hospitals, laundromats, restrooms, sanitariums, rest homes, public campgrounds, doctors' offices, restaurants, conference centers, jails, phone booths, bookstores, nursing homes, truck stops, motels, information centers, homes, churches, airports, markets, milkhouses, trade fairs, stores, bleachers, city streets, and subways.

Just for You is distributed in dozens of ways.

Some shut-ins with limited opportunities to contact others have a distribution ministry by mail. Some groups maintain a mailing list covering their city. Others personally distribute literature from door to door. Youth groups frequently distribute it as a monthly activity. One family imprints their church name on the paper and takes responsibility to distribute it in the community.

Pastors use it in personal visitation and draw from its content in sermon preparation. It has also been used as a source for quotes in local newspapers and radio programs.

Some individuals hand it to callers at their own homes, and some order a supply especially to take when they travel away from home. Some businesses enclose it with employee pay checks and customer mailings. And some customers enclose it with mail sent to businesses.

Matthew Shoemaker in the first CLE warehouse in Building No. 1. Full-length walkways between tiers of shelves were designed as elevators to reach every level of the floor-to-ceiling storage.

Just for You *is appreciated by many who receive it.*

"I picked up a folder left on my car. . . . I would like to be on your mailing list."

"By mistake the mailman delivered one to the wrong box. I want it for myself."

A lady who found one on her gate wrote:

> I wish you'd send these same pamphlets to my half-brother and his wife. Thank you for the pamphlets. I know not where they come from, but I thank God for them and hope they will continue to arrive at my home and my brother's home too.

Just for You *is easy to distribute.*

One regular distributor wrote:

> I have found *Just for You* the easiest tract that I know of to give to the public.
>
> One day I knocked on a screen door (the main door was open) and saw a lady approaching. When she saw me standing there with a paper in my hand, a very evident frown crossed her face. When she got closer to the door, I held up the *Just for You* so she could plainly see the heading, and said, "Just for you." The frown left and smiling she said, "Just for me?" and I returned, "Yes, just for you." She

unhooked the screen door, took the paper, and said, "Thank you" in a very pleasing manner.

*Regular distributors of **Just for You** recommend an imprint.*
Many imprints include only a church or family name along with an address and an invitation to services or a number to call for spiritual help. Here is one example of an imprint that carries an additional message:

Do you need someone to love you?
Here is the answer:
God is love. 1 John 4:8

If you want someone to help you
understand God's love, contact:
(name and address)

Jose Liscano translates Just for You *into the Spanish edition called* Para Ti. Para Ti *is regularly published every two months and is available free of charge on an individual or bulk subscription basis.*

31

Just for You *is free of charge.*

The hundreds of written responses are a humbling reminder that *Just for You* is one of CLP's most far-reaching ministries. CLP sends the pamphlet free of charge as single copies or in bulk and will continue to do so as resources are available.

Many distributors are not in a position to pay for the quantities they order, and many who have resources are not as able to distribute. So by working together, the ministry can go on.

Just for You *is effective.*

Here are some personal testimonies from users:

One man from New York wrote, "I thank God for many commitments to Christ as a result of *Just for You*'s sent to me, and my giving them out."

Another said, "The *Just for You* tracts that you sent us for our Prison Revival in July were a great asset to our efforts in winning souls for Christ. The inmates enjoy reading this type of Christian material."

From England came this testimony:

> I use these tracts in street witnessing; they are very popular here in Broadstairs, with young and old alike. People are always willing to take one and read it, as they

CLP employees helped to pay for this billboard sign near Harrisonburg.

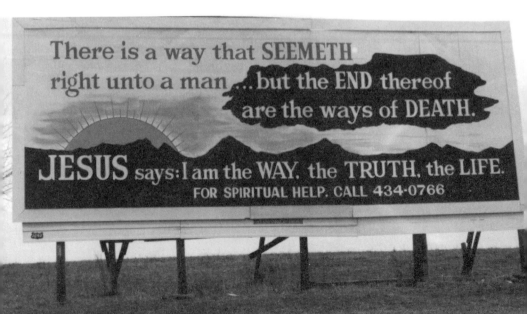

look attractive and are interesting. Many people of all ages are getting saved on the streets, so thank you again!"

Thousands of *Just for You* tracts have been distributed in Africa, and many encouraging replies have come back. For example:

"I have many testimonies to give concerning this publication [Just for You], which cannot contain this mail. All I know is that Christ has changed and renewed me spiritually through this medium. My friends are giving the same testimony. In fact, I must say that you are really making disciples of Christ in Nigeria. Keep it up!"

A Special Testimony

A tract evangelist in Hagerstown, Maryland, offered a *Just for You* to a passerby. The man scowled and replied, "I don't care about that stuff."

"Maybe you'd better," replied the evangelist pleasantly.

With that the man retraced his steps and demanded the tract. Taking the *Just for You* defiantly in his one hand, he thrust his other hand into his pocket and withdrew a lighter. He flicked the lighter and held it to the corner of the tract. The flame  touched the paper and promptly went out. The man relit the lighter, and raised it again to the same place. The flame again immediately went out. This procedure was repeated at least six times.

Finally, in a voice filled with surprise, the evangelist said, "You know, I don't believe you can burn it!"

"Oh, yes I can," the man replied. Then placing his fingers between the leaves of the paper, he again held the lighter to them. This time the leaves did catch fire, but burned very temporarily and again flickered out.

Two *Just for You*'s had been put together, the one inside the other. When the corner of the first burned off, a bold red "You" showed from the second one.

Condemned, the man thrust the paper back into the hands of the evangelist and strode away.

The Lord has a jealousy for the witness of His name!

Arrive Alive

In 1972 a special issue of *Just for You* entitled *Arrive Alive* was distributed for the first time. This brochure, with an attractive, full-color photo on the front, has been widely distributed both in the United States and England. Many Chambers of Commerce have displayed it with their travel brochures.

The first printing of 35,000 in 1972 was followed two months later by a printing of 54,000, and in another three months with 60,000. The largest single printing was 300,000 in 1976. To date there have been ten printings with a total of more than 1,000,000 copies.

Arrive Alive encourages not only safe driving, but also safe living that leads to heaven. The brochure includes a coupon that may be returned for more literature. Hundreds of requests have come for literature on salvation, assurance, various Bible doctrines, or some personal need.

Arrive Alive has brought much encouraging correspondence to the office. One lady from Chicago who wrote for more literature added this comment: "I was thrilled to pick up this particular tract at a gas station rack while on our way to Minnesota." Since her coupon had been imprinted by a Wisconsin Chamber of Commerce, we passed her comment on to them, and they wrote a letter of thanks, stating, "We also have received a letter and comments from others on the *Arrive Alive* folder. We have around 50 copies on hand and will distribute more if they are available." This particular Chamber of Commerce received hundreds of brochures in several shipments.

From New York came this encouraging report: "Your tract entitled *Arrive Alive* is a *dynamic* tract. My husband and I are putting it in an airport rack and they are going fast. Could you send me 500 more?"

Arrive Alive tracts (as well as all follow-up literature) are sent free of charge upon request. Costs are taken care of through freewill offerings from some who distribute and from many others who are interested in helping make distribution possible. Although CLP is no longer specifically advertising this leaflet, quantity orders continue to come in.

One distributor who recently ordered 4,000 *Arrive Alive* wrote, "Please pray for our Gospel tract ministry. A few have been saved." And CLP sends that same request. Please pray for the thousands who have been encouraged to "arrive alive" at the end of life's journey, ready to live forever in fullness of joy with our Lord.

From an Employee

Little did I realize on that June day in 1972 that the Lord would lead me to continue on at CLP for well over twenty years. I was hired, as I recall, to write a social studies text among other assignments. My intent was to move on after completing the project.

As it turned out, I had the opportunity to work on social studies, edit *Companions*, write a study guide on nonconformity, and take on numerous other challenging projects.

One great blessing in working at CLP has been the privilege of working in a Christian environment, apart from the influence of ungodly language, music, and actions.

Another blessing has been that of working with Christian literature in a way that directly influences the lives of others for Christ. I am convinced that this opportunity has made me more conscious of witnessing in other areas including farming, my second occupation.

Undoubtedly the greatest blessings I have received from working at CLP are the inspirational testimonies of those who have been blessed by using the material and especially the encouragement of those who have come to the Mennonite faith because of what they have read. I have experienced the challenge and the blessing of I Corinthians 15:58: "Be ye stedfast, unmoveable, always abounding in the work of the Lord, forasmuch as ye know that your labour is not in vain in the Lord." —Roger Berry

---
From an Employee

The Lord was guiding my life when I came to work at CLP. I had been a widow for three years. I was needing a better car and wanted a job to pay for it—it had to be part-time because I had five teenage children living at home. I had listened to a relative talk about CLP when she worked there and knowing some people working there, I filled out an application for work. This would be helping in the Lord's work as well as meeting my own needs. Several months later a good car was available for me and I agreed to buy it. That same day I got a call from CLP to come to work. Praise the Lord for His timing!

I have continued to serve here 15 years which has brought spiritual and material blessings. We are like a big Christian family here, working together to give God's message to all the world.   —Eva Sonifrank Glanzer

---

Social Studies Series

The publication of the first social studies book, *Living Together on God's Earth,* in 1974 was a small step toward a totally Christian curriculum, but it seemed a big step for CLP. Since that time three more books have come out in the social studies series, and two are in the making.

Third grade: *Living Together on God's Earth*, 1974, by John Martin
Fourth grade: *Into All the World*, 1991, by Roger Berry
Fifth grade: *North America Is the Lord's*, 1980, by James Lowry
Sixth grade: Latin America (needing a writer)
Seventh grade: *God's World, His Story*, 1976, by Roger Berry
Eighth grade: U.S. History (in beginning stage)

Special difficulties attend the production of such books. First, the full-color pictures and detailed maps are expensive to produce. Second, the work of the writer in researching and gathering material and organizing it seems monumental. Third, the world political scene is so volatile that text information may be outdated before it is published. For example, when the manuscript for *Into All the World* was nearly complete, East and West Germany announced they were merging. Maps and data for Europe were immediately out of date and text needed to be rewritten. The book was finally released in 1992.

Nonetheless, the significance of a Christian social studies series has given impetus to keep this venture going. Why is social studies so important? The answer to this question is well-stated in the introduction to the seventh grade book:

> The social studies represents a particularly crucial course in the school curriculum. This is because such a study teaches young people social values which help build a philosophy of life. . . .
>
> The standard social studies textbooks of today are humanistic. They are man-centered. They assume that man is innately good, and that through the persistent efforts of modern science, he will eventually solve all of his problems. According to this philosophy, the world is moving toward a utopia where man will have learned to coexist in an uninterrupted peace. The cancer of this demonic philosophy has crept from the classroom into the Christian church, and we have seen only the beginning of the havoc to follow in

Eva Glanzer working on the CCI phototypesetting system in the old composition room.

Doris Greider operating the NCR—CLP's first computer system.

the form of arrogant individualism, disrespect for Biblical authority and traditional values, and a situation approach to ethics.

The most modern social studies texts now boldly assert the concepts of humanism that were peddled only cautiously in the textbooks of yesterday. Alarmed by these emboldened attacks on the roots of society and Christian faith, Christian Light Publications has been moved by God to the preparation of a social studies curriculum based upon the revealed value system of God's Word.

In 1974, when the first social studies book came out, CLP received this word of encouragement from a user:

> Some quite good textbooks come in very ordinary nondescript, workday covers. Some have interesting covers but dry, uninteresting "interiors." How delightful to receive a copy of a new textbook with a lovely, inviting cover and chapters inside just begging to be read!
>
> Surely you can't fully realize what a good thing God has

enabled you to place in our hands. We trust that it is the first fruit of many more to come.

Someone has said that a good book can be picked up with expectancy and put down with profit. Thank you for a good book!

Another wrote:

We are *very* pleased with "Living Together on God's Earth" and feel it is an excellent attempt at presenting Social Studies to intermediate students with a truly Biblical perspective.

But . . . do you have anything for the junior high grades? I'm sitting at my desk just viewing the Social Studies series that our school has for this coming school year, and after looking at your book I'm thoroughly disgusted with the one we plan to use this coming school year.

Please reply to my question quickly, as I would like to hold off sending for workbooks until I have done a good job of checking out Christian series.

Responses like these to the first book spurred CLP on to publish more in the social studies series. Some of the most challenging testimonies have been from parents who have described how the Lord used their children's books in their own lives.

One lady telephoned from several thousand miles away to ask, "Does anyone in my area practice what this book teaches?" The office was able to direct her to a conservative Mennonite church where she later became a member. Writing specifically of the social studies book, she says, "Little did I realize that the reading of this book would literally turn my life around. My perspective on patriotism, politics, and pacifism [nonresistance] was the exact opposite of the author's."

Another lady had this to say:

A few years ago when my daughter was in homeschool, I used your curriculum for her seventh grade classes. . . . I was especially impressed by her Social Studies book entitled

Lula Showalter putting hardcase binding on North America Is the Lord's.

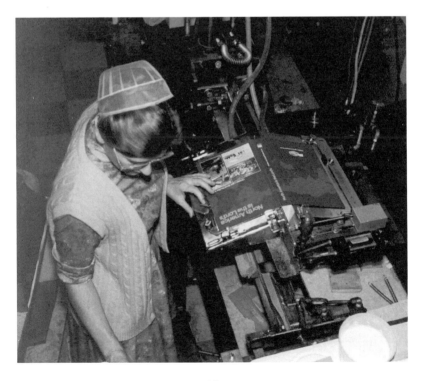

Mary Catherine Showalter, bookkeeper at work. 1977

God's World, His Story. I think that was the most interesting and informative book I have ever read. I think that as the teacher, I learned more than my student. I loved the way it tied history to the Bible. It helped me understand God's prophecies more fully!

Eventually, my daughter returned to public school because her father was ill and my every moment was spent in caring for him. At that time, I gave all her textbooks to a friend who is also a homeschool mother. I was delighted that she could use them, of course, but I have been lost without that book! Therefore, please send me an order form and price list so I may purchase another.

One pastor from Massachusetts wrote that he was using the fifth grade textbook in junior high. He explained:

We are aware that the book was prepared for use at a lower level; however, there is such a dearth of Christian texts in this subject area that we are using it with supplementary reading. The students seem to be challenged.

And so is CLP! The work at times seems overwhelming, but it is humbling and encouraging to see the Lord bringing the right materials to the right people at just the right time.

Part III: Christian Light Education, 1979-

[The LORD] established a testimony in Jacob, and appointed a law in Israel, which he commanded our fathers, that they should make them known to their children: That the generation to come might know them, even the children which should be born; who should arise and declare them to their children: That they might set their hope in God, and not forget the works of God, but keep his commandments (Psalm 78:5-7).

"God's truth equipping God's people to do God's work."

Appearing on the cover of every LIGHTUNIT, the above represents the philosophy of CLE for the entire world.

By far the largest venture of CLP came with the development of Christian Light Education. Sanford Shank's vision for a Christian school curriculum went back at least to his college days. As he sat in class after class preparing for elementary education, he observed the many teachings in popular elementary textbooks that were contrary to Christian faith. Sanford's professor, however, said there was no way a Christian publisher could compete with secular publishers in producing a quality school curriculum. The best alternative, he advised, was for Christian teachers to point out the erroneous teaching in secular textbooks.

Sanford remained unconvinced. Years later, his views were

articulated in an article that appeared in *Alight* and *Parent Lines.*

Our Children—A Mission

We take our families to church to be nurtured in the faith, and we should do that. It is an important aspect of our responsibility to ourselves and our children.

We send missionaries to other countries to tell the lost about Christ, and we should do that too. It is an important aspect of the church's responsibility.

We give our children schooling to train them for life, and it is right that we should. It is important that they acquire the knowledge and skills necessary for a successful kingdom-building vocation.

Sanford Shank , CLE Director, usually checked
LIGHTUNITs the final time before they were printed.

But it seems strange that so many people who would support and promote missions are apparently unconcerned when their own children are absorbing ideas that lead away from the truth. Their children are being prepared to succeed in the world, but not to be faithful builders of the church in the world.

Our children are one of the largest mission fields. These children we have brought into the world can go with us into heaven if they choose the right way. Realizing the importance of leading them to the right choice, we must provide materials that teach our children truth. If we want our children to be Christians, we must provide Christian training.

Notwithstanding the help of the church and the Christian school, parents are ultimately responsible for the training of their children. They need to weigh carefully how their children are being influenced at school—six hours a day, 180 days per year. While we recognize the value of godly teachers, we dare not minimize the far-reaching influence of a sound school curriculum in shaping our children's destinies.

Many respond to appeals for funds that will clothe and feed the cold and hungry, and rightly so. *But if it is important to care for these bodies which are intended to last only a lifetime, isn't it even more important to feed and clothe the souls which will live eternally? How much more we should be stirred by the needs of people who suffer everlasting torments of fire and thirst.* We cannot help them, but we can help keep others from such doom.

We do not minimize the need for worldwide missions, but we would also emphasize that souls at home are no less important in God's sight than souls in foreign lands. And providing a sound nurture program at home is our *first* responsibility.

Christian Light Education (CLE) for grades one through twelve was developed out of this conviction for a doctrinally sound school curriculum.

Negotiations With ACE

As early as 1973 a report was given to the CLP Board about the Accelerated Christian Education (ACE) curriculum begun in Texas a couple of years earlier. This approach to curriculum seemed more attainable than a complete curriculum of hardcover texts. But although the idea was reviewed, several years passed before more steps were taken.

Meanwhile reports came that Mennonite and Amish schools were using ACE. This approach to education was growing. As public schools deteriorated, more Christian schools were being established. Many of them were small and found it difficult to carry on a full program. The ACE materials were largely self-instructional, allowing every student to work at his own level and pace, and making it possible for one teacher to handle the demands of a wide range of grades more easily. On a number of significant points, however, ACE materials differed from Mennonite theology. Concern was expressed not only about the curriculum's impact on school children, but the impact on teachers who were being trained under the ACE organization.

In 1977, the CLP Board decided that representatives from CLP should meet with the head of the ACE organization to explore the possibility of revising their curriculum for the CLP constituency. Although this meeting was congenial, the CLP Board and their advisors felt the terms of the contract were too restrictive.

When CLP presented the idea of revising an existing curriculum to a large group of ordained brethren in a nationwide meeting, the consensus was to move ahead only if CLP could have full control of curriculum content and teacher training.

Tim Korver operating the Royal Zenith 2-color press.

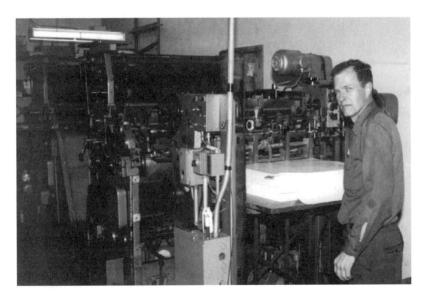

From an Employee

After a year and a half of working at Christian Light Publications, I can say that I am overjoyed at the opportunity to come here to work each day. It is a highlight of my life to be able to share in the work of publishing Christian literature.

One of the many blessings I enjoy in working here at CLP is the daily experience of being with other Christians—Christians who come from different settings and experiences and so add color and dimension to my Christian experience. From past occupations I know what it is to be in a situation where I was nearly always at odds in moral decisions. Praise God for the fellowship of the saints that encourages and strengthens convictions.

I count it a real privilege to share with friends the progress and challenges of the work at CLP. I am trusting the Lord to continue to bless the work here and am looking forward to many enriching times in my labors here.

—Timothy Korver

Alpha Omega Publications

About this time someone gave CLP information about Alpha Omega Publications, which was then in its first years of producing a curriculum similar to ACE. Discussions with AOP eventually led to a satisfactory contract in which CLP had rights to revise AOP's curriculum and reproduce it for their own use.

In the fall of 1979, Paul Hartman provided a large closed truck, and CLP purchased a machine for making prints economically. Using the back of the truck as their workshop, Paul and Sanford Shank spent more than two weeks at the AOP headquarters in Tempe, Arizona, making prints from original layouts. Members of the Berean Mennonite Church in Phoenix also helped, especially Joe and Lottie Miller, who parked their camper close to the truck and provided meals in addition to helping with the print making. By alternating work and rest periods, the team was able to work pretty well around the clock and completed the task in record time. CLP is indeed grateful for the donation of time and materials, for the

Kristin (Hobbs) Good and Wilma Rohrer worked many late nights pasting revisions on the CLE layout sheets.

services of Paul and various members of the Berean congregation, and for the hospitality of AOP during this time. CLP is especially indebted to AOP for making the layouts available.

Adapting an existing curriculum had numerous advantages for CLP, a major one being the tremendous financial savings. Millions of dollars and thousands of hours are normally spent by large companies in planning and developing curriculum. Without millions of dollars and thousands of hours to spend, CLP took AOP's offer as the Lord's answer to a pressing need.

Even so, the work ahead loomed like a huge mountain. Individualized learning centers would need the complete program. Each year's delay in putting the whole package on the market would mean much greater cost. There could be no income without sales, no sales without the product, and no advantageous way to market only part of the program.

Production of CLE Curriculum

When the Board decided in November of 1978 to move ahead as the way opened with personnel and finances, CLP shifted into high gear and worked toward producing the material as rapidly as possible. Christian Light Publications created a special division to handle this new venture: Christian Light Education (CLE).

One of the first steps was to publicize the estimated needs—100 people and $600,000 (beyond regular operating expenses needed for the ongoing work of the organization). The Lord worked through His people! The August 1979 newsletter stated there were 90-100 people working on curriculum. "It seemed almost miraculous the way responses came in for personnel this summer," the newsletter reported. The Lord also moved many people to share in donations. Although the total amount was not received at the beginning, the Board felt CLE should move ahead in faith. They felt a kinship with Joshua and the Children of Israel crossing the Jordan River. Not until the priests' feet came to the water, did the Israelites see the miraculous deliverance of the Lord.

What happened in the next two years was possible only through the hand of the Lord and the cooperation of hundreds of people. Words cannot adequately convey the feelings and hard work packed into hours of planning, decision making, meetings, and letter writing, and the hard labor on the part of reviewers, revisors, writers, artists, editorial committees, scheduling persons, typesetters, proofreaders, pressmen, and later, those in ordering, shipping, and bookkeeping departments.

Early in 1979 a new section was added to the press facilities especially to accommodate new equipment for printing and binding. This also provided new space for layout and mailing. An adjoining area was adapted for storage of the 600 different worktexts that made up the basic CLE curriculum. Finding an area for storage exactly the right size, located at exactly the right spot to join the new mailing room did not seem like a coincidence. The Lord surely knew the future when that area had been built seven years earlier. It was

Donna (Ropp) Beery spent many hours typesetting CLE LIGHTUNITS.

Sterling Shank reviewing a LIGHTUNIT. Reviewers worked through LIGHTUNITs and suggested changes for Revisors to consider.

exactly the right size for the shelving that held the twelve levels, each with the right amount of space.

The new addition was essential, but its construction added its load to an already tight schedule and overworked staff. It also made its contribution of noise, clutter, and commotion to the workplace. Funds for this building, however, were not taken from contributions to curriculum development or operating expenses.

Also during the late summer of 1979, fifteen teachers and administrators took teacher training in preparation to begin individualized learning centers during the 1979-80 school year. One part of the curriculum ready for field testing that year was the first grade material. Orpha Tice, a first grade teacher for many years, developed the *Learning to Read* program and replaced AOP's first grade curriculum with

Ward Beachy and Ruth Martin collating books on the saddleback stitcher.

original CLE material.

By early 1980 production was in full swing, although revision was still being done. The goal was to have beginning books ready for the beginning of the 1980-81 school year, then continue to produce LIGHTUNITs in time to fill orders as needed throughout the school year.

It would not be truthful to give the impression that there were no problems in carrying out this plan or that schools had no frustrations because of it. There were plenty of both. But what a blessing were those sympathetic users who not only accepted irregularities in schedule, but who took this first printing of materials, noted errors, and helped CLE find what needed further revision before subsequent printings.

From an Employee

It really has been a good experience working with you all this past year. Thank you for the stimulating, interesting experiences. We as a family have made many friends that we treasure. May the Lord richly bless you as you continue serving Him. Remember us in your prayers and write us about the things that happen in your pilgrimages.

—Dwight Beachy

[Dwight Beachy moved with his family from North Dakota to Harrisonburg for one year to help with the revision of AOP material.]

From an Employee

It has been a pleasure to work among you full-time or part-time for the past two years. I'm sure I will often think about you and the work here. I want to continue praying for you. I would also appreciate your prayers for me as I serve the Lord in Puerto Rico.

Thank you so much for the gift, *Apples of Gold*. It looks interesting.

—Orpha Tice

[After developing the first grade materials for CLE, Orpha Tice moved to Puerto Rico to teach in a mission school.]

Orpha Tice wrote CLE's original Learning to Read program and helped with the secretarial work involved in marketing and shipping curriculum materials.

The First School Year

During the spring and summer of 1980, approximately 250 teachers and administrators in nine different training weeks received hands-on introduction to CLE curriculum, its policies and procedures. More than 100 schools and homes received curriculum for grades 1-12 in the fall of 1980.

In addition to revising AOP materials, CLE replaced some AOP material with original curriculum. First grade, for example, was fully replaced. In addition, CLE used its own social studies series on the levels available, and continues to replace as new social studies textbooks are published.

The Lord sends rewards in various ways, but one reward of publishing is finding that published material has met the needs of its users. Here is how one CLE teaching principal expressed his feelings:

> Why did we choose the Christian Light Education curriculum? First of all, we were looking for a conservative Anabaptist curriculum with a full twelve-year school program. Christian Light Education has more than fulfilled our expectations in this area, not only having a conservative Anabaptist approach to teaching the Bible, but throughout the curriculum even down to the illustrations and various examples from everyday life used in math problems. We

appreciate this viewpoint which directs the student into a wholesome Christian life and away from the humanistic and materialistic philosophies of today's world.

Second, the individual learning concept appealed to us since one staff person could teach a wider grade span and more subjects at the upper grade levels. It would be next to impossible for one teacher to handle this many high school students, including various electives, in a conventional setting without severely sacrificing quality. . . .

As we have seen our basic reasons for the CLE program fulfilled and exceeded and have seen the many added benefits of CLE helping educate our students for eternity, we are extremely grateful.

From an Employee

"And we know that all things work together for good to them that love God, to them who are the called according to his purpose" (Romans 8:28).

It seems like only yesterday when I filled out the detailed application, mailed it, and tried to patiently await a reply. The reply didn't come according to *my* plans but God worked it out. Now three-fourths of my one-year VS term is history. One of the many blessings I'm experiencing is working with other Christians. May the printed word always be permitted to be sent forth to touch hearts and lives of people everywhere.

—Willodean Martin

Star Revision

Following the original revision, which dealt primarily with doctrinal matters, the second printing corrected errors and improved exercises and test questions. In order to further improve academic quality, a major Star Revision was begun in 1983.

This revision process included review of volunteer students' workbooks from a variety of schools. Participating schools received credit for free LIGHTUNITs to replace those they returned for Star Revision. Since the plan was to have Star Revision completed by the time second printing was used up, those levels with the heaviest usage were revised first. In the fall of 1985 the first Star Revision LIGHTUNITs were available, and by 1989 most of the Star Revision objectives had been completed for the elementary levels. Because fewer copies of high school materials are sold, they have been the last to be revised. In this third revision a number of LIGHTUNITs were completely rewritten to replace ones that were weak.

The Quality of CLE

In preparing students academically, CLE has sought to help students gain insight in keeping with Proverbs 4:7: "Wisdom is the principal thing, therefore get wisdom: and with all thy getting get understanding." Throughout the curriculum, students are taught to think and to evaluate in order to lead them to an understanding of concepts.

How successful has CLE actually been in providing a quality education for children? CLE certainly is not flawless, and revision and improvement continue to be part of the ongoing vision. Responses from users, however, have been very encouraging.

Sterling Beachy, Shop Foreman, working at the platemaker. Final layout pages are burned onto metal or photodirect plastic plates for the press. Offset printing designates the method of printing by using these plates which, when placed on the press, will offset the printing to a rubber blanket in reverse type. The paper is printed as it is pressed between rollers and passes over the blanket.

John Swartz, Director of CLE Curriculum Development, does much work from his home in West Virginia.

From Our Users

One user had this to say: "After using CLE almost five years, we can testify that it is a superior curriculum. We have been well pleased with the results we see in our children."

From Canada we had this encouragement:

Our children scored the highest of the home-schoolers in Manitoba. They are tested yearly by the Department of Education to assure that we are properly educating them. We felt it really spoke loud and clear for the Christian Light material.

Another Canadian user reported that the visiting Elementary Grade Supervisor suggested she change to CLE.

A mother whose son went to public school for grade nine after using CLE since second grade had this to say:

We just want to thank you for an excellent curriculum that teaches so much more than just academic material. And the academic material is excellent, too. Our son's history teacher commented that he can tell our son is very literate and has read history material not generally taught in school. He liked his fresh, informed answers and hopes to have him in one of his classes all four years. (Social studies was by far his favorite subject.)

Another factor indicating satisfactory academic quality is the success of CLE students who go on to college. The Director of Admissions for a college in New England wrote: "We are pleased to notify you that one of your advisees is the recipient of an Academic

Achievement Scholarship from our college. . . . Such a fine student is a credit to your school."

CLE is concerned about academic quality and grateful for these reports. But is academic quality the most important feature of a Christian curriculum? What is God's standard for judging quality? Solomon declared, "The fear of the LORD is the beginning of wisdom" (Proverbs 9:10a). God surely will judge the quality of any curriculum on the basis of whether or not it instills the fear of the Lord. The concern for doctrinal soundness of faith that leads to obedience in life is one of the primary factors that brought CLE into existence.

Many CLE users are looking for that kind of quality. One said it this way:

> We would like to thank you for your assistance in making it possible for our daughter to have the high quality of education we feel she has gotten from your material (as evidenced by her achievement test scores). More than that you provided the spiritual material that will enable her to use her knowledge the proper way. We have seen great changes in her these past two years. Bible was her favorite subject.

Rachel Friesen preparing a package for shipping.

Bethany Hartzler, engaged to Kevin Shank, processing stacks of inquiries from potential customers asking for information and samples of CLE curriculum.

After expressing appreciation for a science LIGHTUNIT, one parent wrote:

> I might also add by way of encouragement to you a comment on 6th level Social Studies. . . . Two weeks ago at regular Sunday services, the brother who ministered traced the finger of God through the peoples of history very much like it is presented in your textbook. Our daughter recognized and was thrilled by the historical facts coupled with Scripture. It all came alive to her! We see the value of a God-based curriculum!

From a Reviewer

Following are excerpts from a review given by a non-Mennonite, nationally recognized educator:

> Christian Light Education was established in 1979 as a part of the ministry of Christian Light Publications, a provider of school materials that emphasize a literal

57

Sue Byler, who has worked in the computer/order department since 1987, takes many of the CLE orders that come by telephone.

understanding and practical application of the Scriptures. While the materials are prepared from an Anabaptist-Mennonite perspective, they have received very positive acceptance by many others. . . .

Christian Light offers a worktext approach, based on their own revision of the very popular Alpha Omega worktexts. Christian Light's revised texts are more attractive than the original, with heavy kivarlike paper covers and colored ink used within. As revised, their curriculum is more down-to-earth; family-centered stories replace AOP's fantasy stories in the lower grades, for example. Pictures reflect Mennonite community values: women have uncut, covered hair; dress is very modest; we see nice large families.

Christian Light incorporates several of its own hardcover textbooks and a few other resource books into the program. . . .

Religious orientation is gently Mennonite (they don't beat you over the head with it). Traditional family values and sexual roles are stressed. The curriculum is creationist,

David Miller, full-time, in-house artist since 1988 works at his specially designed art table.

pacifist, and determinedly nonpolitical.

The curriculum emphasizes the basic skills as well as offering a strong program in science and social studies. First grade starts with the intensive phonics Learning to Read program, which is easy to teach and very inexpensive. As a whole, this largely self-contained curriculum stresses thinking skills. . . .

The original Alpha Omega materials are very good in English and science, and Christian Light hasn't hurt these areas any. The social studies emphasis is different, reflecting Mennonite concerns. I consider Christian Light's changes to the early-grade's materials to be an improvement.

Christian Light sells all needed materials for its science courses. . . . This places their science program head and shoulders above most others. . . .

Children can progress rapidly with Christian Light's material, and they will truly learn how to learn. Academically, I give Christian Light an A.

For those favoring Mennonite religious and political beliefs, Christian Light is a "best buy."

How Was CLE Funded?

CLE saved tremendous cost by the cooperation of AOP in providing the basic curriculum and originals for prints which could be revised with a minimum of production time. Many more savings came through the cooperation and participation of a large number of people who donated their time or worked at a lower-than-standard wage. Calculating the production costs on the basis of a national printing estimate chart and the estimates of a national textbook publisher, CLE should have cost around two million dollars. Instead, the actual cost was less than one million.

Donations came in satisfactorily to cover initial development for the first year. About that time, production was moving into full swing and costs were escalating. . . and then donations began to taper off. CLP faced the soul-searching dilemma: *Shall we stop or go forward? If we go on, how will we do it?*

Repeatedly, advisors responded, "Don't quit now. We want the material." Some suggested that people support a project better when they see the finished product: "Get it on the market. Then people will see what they are paying for." Although CLP was advised to borrow money, they first considered other alternatives, such as producing a partial curriculum.

The question of borrowing funds, however, came back. Advice was mixed. Different people have different ideas about borrowing money. When CLP's needs were made known, numerous offers came from the brotherhood of money available on loan, either at no interest or at low interest rates.

Grace Lahman at work in her home giving LIGHTUNIT layouts a quality check after first proofreading and corrections have been made.

The CLP Board grappled with this question. Borrowed money needs to be repaid. They believed that God's people should be willing to invest money in kingdom-building projects. Yet they realized that some people with great interest in helping

60

Charles Hoff checking CLE orders. Orders received by mail or telephone are first entered into the computer in the Order Department. From the packing list sent to the shipping room, each order is pulled from inventory and placed in an open tray which is moved by roller track to the checking station. The checker will enter into the computer each item in the tray and the computer will then compare and note any discrepancies between the record of the pulled order and the original order as first entered.

depended on income from their investments to provide for their personal needs. After prayerful consideration, the Board accepted borrowed funds as the Lord's provision to meet the needs of curriculum production.

Not everyone agreed with the decision of the Board. CLP is grateful, however, for the continued support of the constituency. Some of the loans became gifts. Some mistakenly thought that once the product was on the market, sales would adequately cover the costs. Unfortunately, this is not the case. If development costs were included in the selling price, Christian schools and homeschools could not afford to buy the material. The financial need, therefore, is ongoing, and again, CLP is grateful to the many who share this vision and to those whom the Lord stirs up to support it financially.

In the fourteen years since CLE has been available, many at CLP

Naomi Myers (right) and Eva Glanzer proofreading as a team with Eva reading from original manuscript and Naomi comparing typeset copy with what is being read.

Christian Light Education display showing the approximately 600 LIGHTUNITs and several hardcover texts that make up the curriculum for Grades 1-12. The curriculum includes 5 subject areas—Bible, Language Arts, Math, Social Studies, and Science—plus Learning to Read and 18 different electives. Display also includes teacher training, parent orientation LIGHTUNITs, and various teacher's manuals. (Picture taken in CLP's front display room in 1989.)

have reflected on the task of curriculum production. Can a Christian publisher produce quality curriculum? Are there people qualified for such work? Strictly from the human standpoint many even at CLP, in spite of testimonies from satisfied users, would feel like saying no. The cry of the Apostle Paul seems more fitting: "Who is sufficient for these things?" (II Corinthians 2:16). But with genuine humility and overwhelming gratitude to the Lord, God's people can go on to say with Paul, "And such trust have we through Christ to God-ward: Not that we are sufficient of ourselves to think any thing as of ourselves; but our sufficiency is of God" (II Corinthians 3:4, 5).

From an Employee

Have you ever felt that life was getting "in a rut," that you really weren't accomplishing what God wanted you to, that maybe He had something else for you to do? I have felt that way, that God was calling me to service, but where and to what? No doors seemed to open for me. I didn't hear Him say "Go," so I resolved to wait on His timing to show me when and where.

In the meantime I learned of the need at CLP for workers, but for a long time things just didn't seem to work out. Many questions arose in my mind. (1) I didn't have the finances for the trip from my home in Oregon to Virginia. (2) How about my obligation to my parents? The rest of the family? (3) I had been dating a girl from our church . . . how would a term of service affect our relationship? (4) I was working part-time for a local tire shop, and the boss wanted me to stay for several more months at least. I just asked the Lord to work things out according to His will. Then, in a span of several months, one by one my questions were answered, the doors seemed to open, and I was off to CLP.

One of the things I enjoy most at CLP is working for and with people who love the Lord deeply and who have a burden for those around them. This is an important challenge to me, along with the fact that I am helping to make God's Word available in printed form, which reaches out to lives that seemingly are hardened against the Gospel.

As far as my work is concerned, my jobs are varied—everything from errands and cleaning to construction to running a press.

Is the Lord calling you to serve Him, and you're not sure where? Ask Him to show you, be willing to wait for His guidance, and consider CLP! The time is short, the need urgent, the promise sure.

"Ask, and it shall be given you; seek, and ye shall find; knock, and it shall be opened unto you: For every one that asketh receiveth; and he that seeketh findeth; and to him that knocketh it shall be opened" (Matthew 7:7, 8).

—Joe Strubhar

CLE and Park View Press

Producing CLE materials called for printing procedures on a scale Park View Press had not known heretofore. New equipment was purchased and installed. Sanford Shank, founder of both organizations, believed the printer should be a servant to the publisher. This included trying to find the most economical ways for CLP to get their materials printed.

Beginning in 1982, both organizations agreed that even though Park View Press was printing for CLP basically at their cost, yet it would be a financial advantage if CLP could do its own printing, using its own employees. An arrangement was worked out whereby many of the employees of Park View Press were moved to the CLP payroll and the equipment was shared by the two organizations.

By design Park View Press had already discontinued much of its commercial printing. PVP did, however, continue to provide photocopy, darkroom, and bindery services and to print some books and periodicals for other customers. In 1988, CLP bought the equipment and has continued doing its own printing plus some periodicals for other nonprofit organizations. Park View Press discontinued business completely at that time, after thirty-one years of operation.

CLE Homestudy Growth

One result of the curriculum CLP did not envision when CLE was first produced, was its wide use in homestudy. As homeschooling became an organized movement across the nation, entire new vistas opened for CLE. Requests began coming to display CLE materials at homeschool conventions. From these displays, inquiries began pouring in.

In 1987, the Mark Bear family from Idaho spent six weeks traveling over 11,000 miles attending conventions as representatives of CLE. In July of that year, 87 new families joined CLE users, and in August, 181 more families were added. One woman expressed her gratitude for what the CLE materials were doing for her family. Her unsaved husband was helping her son with assignments and with Bible memory work. Her concluding remark was, "I know of five families who are now using your curriculum because I recommended it to them."

By the end of 1990 well over 3,000 homeschools were using CLE

Mark and Evelyn Bear, Kingston, Idaho, coordinate the plans for CLE exhibits at homeschool conventions in an average of 130 locations each year. While Mark and Evelyn have personally exhibited materials on many occasions, the work is accomplished with the help of more than thirty other exhibitors also.

Paul and Ethel Reed in the CLE Homestudy Office. Paul has served since 1979 in different aspects of CLE curriculum planning and development . In more recent years as Homestudy Director, he has coordinated the work of several people in the Homestudy Office. Ethel has assisted her husband since 1985, keeping many of the records on homestudy students and sharing the work of hundreds of telephone calls that come to the office from inquirers wanting information or from CLE users asking for assistance in their homestudy program.

materials. In the 1992 exhibiting season, some 10,000 sample packets were handed to homeschool families in conventions and curriculum fairs in 49 states (Alaska was missed) and four provinces. Sample packets were sent to curriculum fairs in Okinawa, Guam, Japan, and Great Britain. That same year, a record 868 new families were added to those using CLE's materials in homeschools.

Due to this ballooning section of CLE, a special homeschool office was opened at CLP under the management of Paul Reed and his wife Ethel. A special homeschool edition of *LightLines* (CLE's newsletter) was begun in 1988. To better serve homeschoolers, three options were offered. The primary option is the Full Program with the CLE office keeping all records of student achievement. From 1979-1990, seventy-nine students had graduated from the Full Program. The 1991 class had 40 seniors, and with the increasing number of students working at lower levels, the number of graduates continues to grow. In the 1993-94 school year, the number of families on the Full Program was nearing 900, with over 1,800 students. The total number of families using CLE curriculum in varying amounts is over 4,000. The personal services provided by the CLE staff keep the phone lines hot most days.

Families choose to homeschool for a variety of reasons. Three parents in one week cited violence in the schools as their reason for beginning to homeschool. In one school the janitor was killed. In another, an eight-year-old girl was shot in the back. Other parents are alarmed by New Age concepts being taught in the public school. One mother said her ninth grade daughter came home telling about the witchcraft and meditation ideas her teacher was presenting.

Many missionary families use CLE materials for their children. A missionary to Zaire wrote, "We have had to return to Canada due to political unrest. We will be going back to Zaire in one week and CLE homeschooling has allowed us to make these moves with greater stability for our children."

Perhaps the most challenging part of the homeschool division of CLE has been responding to the calls of parents who want help beyond their schooling needs. Countless requests have come for information about what Mennonites believe. Many letters or calls

James Hershberger answers many of the telephone calls on the two lines coming into the Homestudy Office.

Esther Heatwole helps with record keeping in the Homestudy Office.

have come asking whether there is a Mennonite congregation in the area where the homeschooler lives.

From an Employee

"O magnify the LORD with me, and let us exalt his name together" (Psalm 34:3).

To magnify the Lord, we need to lift Him up, promote Him, and show and declare Him to be great. But when we do that, the Lord's enemy will be jealous and bring snares to keep us from magnifying the Lord.

In the Homestudy office at Christian Light, the contacts we have are mostly by phone and letter, but occasionally we also meet customers who come in. . . .

Parents sometimes tell us how in one way or another the curriculum has been of spiritual help to their families. One Canadian mother said, "Establishing family devotions regularly every morning has been an added blessing to our family as a result of CLE."

Requests come to us to pray not only for the educational needs but also for spiritual needs. Mothers sometimes mention unsaved husbands, or parents request prayer for unsaved young people. In these contacts we desire to be of help and

---

encouragement to individuals who are seeking for spiritual stepping stones for themselves and for their families. . . .

I am challenged anew by the responsibility to magnify Christ in my soul, spirit, and body as I have opportunities daily to minister to the needs of homeschoolers. I constantly need the Lord's help to be victorious over the enemy who is jealous when Christ is magnified. —Ethel Reed

The Extension Committee

To handle the many inquiries for spiritual help that came to CLP not only through school materials, but through tracts and other literature, CLP formed an Extension Committee. The Committee responds to inquiries about who Mennonites are and what they believe, as well as where those inquiring could find a Biblical fellowship. These inquiries have come from 37 states, plus Germany and Nigeria. More than 30 calls have come from California and at least 15 from Texas.

In a special report, Lloyd Hartzler, the chairman of the Extension Committee, wrote:

The printed page, particularly *Just for You* and the CLE curriculum, is changing lives from coast to coast in a way that was not envisioned. Little did we realize when we began publishing the school curriculum in the late 70s that we would be able to find so many homes where people are looking for the truth and a Biblical fellowship.

What have been the results? Consider these thrilling examples:

—A young man in the army was experiencing conflict between his Christian faith and his involvement in the military. CLE materials in his home helped crystallize his beliefs. He obtained a discharge from the army, and is now working for CLP.

—A girl who grew up on the streets of Toronto and who hardly knew what love was, now is happy in the Lord and is homeschooling her two children.

—A man who had worked as a security guard has moved with his

Lloyd Hartzler, the first employee on CLP's payroll in 1971, serves as chairman of the Extension Committee. His work often includes long distance calling to contact pastors and to help meet the needs of those who call for spiritual help or inquire for church fellowship.

family into a Mennonite community. He and his wife are now members of a Mennonite church, and he is serving as principal in their Christian day school.

—A former dentist in search of a more Scriptural fellowship moved into the Harrisonburg community with his family. They are members of a local Mennonite church, and he is helping with the CLE curriculum at CLP.

—After a career in the Pentagon, a former naval officer and his family have embraced the truth. He gave up a lucrative job with its retirement benefits and is now happily serving the Lord in the Mennonite church.

The ongoing challenge facing the Extension Committee is reflected in the following letters:

From Colorado:

I am hoping that you can make some recommendation on a God-centered church. Many times I have thought about

70

sitting down and writing this letter. As a home school family we have used your social studies textbooks for three years (they're excellent!) and also obtained other articles through your catalog. We so appreciate the Godly stand you take, so lacking in the church in general these days. In the twelve years we've been married, we have been hard pressed to find a church that takes a stand that matches our convictions. . . . There are times when my soul cries out for a Godly body of believers, one where sin is defined by God's standards. Is there one?

From Michigan:

We have been using the Christian Light curriculum to homeschool our children for two years now. During this time we have come to see that the Mennonite beliefs and way of life are true and the way God would have us to live. Could you tell us please if there is a Mennonite church anywhere near us where we could fellowship and worship?

From California:

Your publications, curriculum, and books spread God's Word, a light that gives fathers, mothers, children, and teachers, guidelines to live the way God/Jesus wants us to live, instead of the New Age mind control programs to block the children from finding Jesus and the Bible. How many die daily not knowing Jesus?

We appreciate the vision and burden you carry and share, to mend our brokenness with our minds and hearts. We thank God for this program and others like it.

From Texas:

After reading several articles and tracts on the covering and going through I Corinthians 11 verse by verse, I've decided to wear a covering. This is practically unheard of in

71

the Dallas-Fort Worth area, and I anticipate much misunderstanding and opposition from family members. I would very much like 10 additional copies of your tract, *The Significance of the Christian Woman's Veiling* in order to give to those who are open to reading it. It may help them understand why I'm wearing a covering. I found this tract in Clay's Bookstore in or near Lancaster County, PA while visiting a friend. Of the many tracts I've read on the subject, I like this one best. Thank you for writing it and making it available to others.

From North Carolina:

I agree very much with the biblical standards of plain dress, but have found it impossible to find patterns for modest dresses for my daughter and myself in "worldly" pattern books.

How do the women of your church make their dresses? Do you have a pattern? If so, may I order one? If not, do you think one of the sisters in your congregation could draw me a picture of how they are sewn?

Elizabeth Hostetter, Receptionist, regularly answers incoming calls on 5 telephone lines, helps walk-in customers, and takes care of many in-house photocopying needs.

It would be an answered prayer to have an acceptable standard of dress. It is frustrating to shop today for modest clothing and I would like to have the issue settled once and for all! There are no Mennonite Churches in our area I could go to for advice on this matter.

From Alabama:

Your material is like a light in the darkness. . . . The Lord will bless you for your boldness in obeying Him. A lot of condemnation is being spoken about our wanting to do God's will in *detail*. We're told we are going too far. For example, now, wearing dresses, wanting to learn about head veilings, etc. But we know to fear God more than man, too.

From Kentucky:

I am writing in hope that you can supply me with more information on Mennonites. When I got the *Just for You* folder, I also got a pamphlet called *Mennonites—Who They Are and What They Believe*. I consider myself a simple Christian. I was raised Catholic but have not practiced that religion for years. I feel a big void in my life and I feel I must get back to my Creator before it is too late.

Any information or direction you can send me would be greatly appreciated.

From Arizona:

We have no fellowship of the Mennonites here that we have been able to find. Presently we attend worship service at a nearby church and have Bible study, or Sunday school, at home. We are planning on ordering Sunday school supplies to assist us in this endeavor.

We would like to join the Mennonite Church. We have found that it has a very solid Biblical foundation and feel confident that this is a church where our family would be able to grow both spiritually and in service.

How these "Macedonian calls" should move God's people! Surely God is calling more people from Mennonite settlements to move out in faith to areas where new church outreaches are needed.

From an Employee

Our faith has been strengthened through all that is involved in leaving home for VS.

We have benefitted from broadened friendships in the new work and church setting.

We have been especially blessed by hearing of families who use the printed material and develop convictions for a more Biblical way of life.

—Wayne and Carol Schwartz

CLE Teacher Training

A small CLE training session was held for a few schools beginning in the fall of 1979. Regular training sessions, however, began in 1980, and that year approximately 250 people took training in Harrisonburg. In the years since then hundreds of teachers,

Training session conducted in Hart, Michigan, 1989, by Pete Peters (on far left).

Group of CLE trainees at Harrisonburg, August 1982.

principals, administrators, school board members, ministers, and homeschool parents from coast to coast and several foreign countries have taken the CLE teacher training. Most of the training has been done in the Harrisonburg area, but outpost training sessions have been held in California, Michigan, Ontario, Manitoba, and Mexico. Some of these sessions were conducted largely in German.

The training sessions today are under the direction of Fred Miller. Pete Peters has been conducting the outpost training sessions. Training includes one week of actual learning center experience, using training LIGHTUNITs covering topics such as philosophy of education, motivation, discipline, learning center procedures, administration, and the Learning to Read program. Many have testified to the benefit of the training materials. One lady wrote:

> I just wanted to write and express how impressed I am with the CLE program and the teacher's training LIGHTUNITs. I've never read any material that presents the Scriptures on child discipline, training, and relationships with such wisdom and understanding of God's Spirit. The character that is stressed is rare indeed, and I pray that God will build this (His) character in me, that I may build it in

my children. It brought tears to my eyes as I read over and studied the pages. I know God is pleased with this program, and I thank Him for showing it to me.

Many homeschool parents take the training by correspondence. One had this to say:

> We are presently using _____ curriculum, and you may wonder why we want to switch at this point since the materials are similar. What we like is (1) the training kit for the teacher, (2) your strong Bible-based standards and goals, and (3) your willingness to help.
>
> We have just gone through [Training] LIGHTUNIT #1 and were blessed and encouraged by it in so many ways. In a world full of humanism and warped perspective and values, it was refreshing and uplifting to read and study the unit. I even shared it with my husband, who enjoyed it just the same! It reassured us that we are not alone and that God's ways are pure and the only way!

CLE Workshops

In the interests of helping CLE schools get started and be successful, special one-day workshops are conducted each fall across the nation. Workshops are designed to provide in-service training, sharing, inspiration, and fellowship for anyone involved in Christian education. In addition to hearing talks and enrolling in sectional workshops, those attending have access to free literature including sample packets, a curriculum exhibit, and books for sale. Often there are question-and-answer sessions and a time to share helpful pointers.

The first CLE workshops were held in the fall of 1980 in Minnesota, Michigan, Maryland, and South Carolina. In the early years, these workshops were held in CLE individualized schools. The workshop team (in addition to conducting the workshops) visited CLE schools to provide counsel, evaluation, and encouragement.

As the workshop ministry has expanded, however, changes have been made. Any place where there is sufficient interest may host a workshop, and anyone is welcome to attend regardless of the curriculum he is using. Registration fees have been discontinued in favor of free-will offerings. Most school visits are now limited to

Sanford Shank and Fred Miller, in the motor home, exchanging ideas between workshop locations.

Teachers and school board members attending a CLE workshop in Quellen Kolonie, near Cuauhtemoc, Mexico in 1983. Their German schools use increasing amounts of CLE English curriculum and Spanish Bible (as it becomes available). Recent permission from CLP to produce a German translation of the CLE curriculum will assist these Kleine Gemeinde Mennonites in ministering to their Old Colony neighbors.

new individualized schools during their first two years with CLE. Sometimes when distance or schedules are prohibitive, the CLE team meets for a time of informal exchange with the new school staff at the fall workshop location.

In some of the more distant locations such as California and Mexico, workshops are scheduled alternately every two years, rather than annually.

Transportation for workshop speakers has improved from a failing Club Wagon to a small motor home. Usually the volunteer driver sleeps during the day while workshops are in session, then drives to the next location during the night. Workshop leaders (often a team of three) have the privilege of being rocked to sleep through the night so that they are ready to begin a new workshop the following morning.

The sentiments of hundreds who attend these workshops annually was summed up by this comment from Indiana:

> I wanted to thank all who were involved with the workshop. It was very helpful and a great encouragement to my husband and myself. . . . Not being Mennonite we were a little apprehensive as to how we would fit in, but that was soon dispelled as we met the people there and were welcomed into one of their homes. We found we had a great deal in common because of the same Spirit that dwells in both of us. It was a real blessing and a learning experience.
>
> The workshop was very good, and we would recommend it for anyone involved with CLE. We learned a great deal about the curriculum and the principles that are built into it. As a homeschool teacher I was able to glean from the messages principles I can apply to my time teaching and to my other children.

Part IV: The Shadow of Death, 1988-1991

LORD, make me to know mine end, and the measure of my days, what it is; that I may know how frail I am. Behold, thou hast made my days as an handbreadth; and mine age is as nothing before thee: verily every man at his best state is altogether vanity (Psalm 39: 4, 5).

The death of Sanford Shank, founder and director of CLP, raises that age-old question in the experience of human suffering and death: Why, Lord? Why take a man at the early age of 56? Why take a man whose lifework seems to stretch ahead so far? Why take the man upon whom so many decisions have depended in the work of Christian Light Publications?

Only as we turn our eyes to that realm that is unseen and to the One who is all-wise can we rest our questions. Out of eternity comes the realization that this life is not the most significant, that earthly accomplishments are not measured by human standards, and that there is a plan larger than CLP's immediate interests, larger than any one person.

Cancer

In February of 1988 Sanford first noticed a knot on his left thigh. Although the first diagnosis was a benign fatty tumor, after surgery it was found to be malignant—liposarcoma, to be exact—one of the most cancerous of cancers. No conventional treatment was known to be effective. There was 100 percent chance that it would return.

Sanford's death less than three years later confirmed the truth of one of his Sunday morning messages following his diagnosis. In this message entitled "The Time Is Short," Sanford described to the Rawley Springs congregation his cancerous condition, but his message was focused on the challenge to be about the Lord's work:

> It is all right to be healthy if God would have it that way. It is good to be happy, but it is better to have the joy of the Lord in your heart. It is good to have needed material things, but it is better to have treasures in heaven. It is good to enjoy life, but enjoying life is an entirely different thing than this world knows. This is a great day to be alive and to be about the Father's business. And this is a great day to die and go to be with the Lord because it will be better.

The second surgery was in November of 1988. The surgeon removed three-fourths of the most powerful muscle in Sanford's thigh and predicted Sanford would need help to walk—at the least a cane. But Sanford recovered and could walk almost normally.

The Sanford Shank family in 1986. Left to right: Sanford, Merna, Miriam (Sterling's wife). Back row: Crystal, Kevin, Sterling.

During 1989 there was no evidence of the cancer. The surgeon, who was not a professing Christian, remarked, "You would make a believer out of an atheist." He was especially impressed with Sanford's attitude.

When the cancer returned again in January of 1990, however, Sanford felt strongly he should not seek further treatment but allow the Lord to work as He deemed best. Sanford asked instead to be anointed with oil, according to the Scripture. After that he just did not feel in his case the Lord would be honored by returning for more surgery.

From January to June the tumor continued to enlarge until it was difficult for Sanford to walk. Beginning July 1, he was mostly bedfast, but he continued to carry on some daily business and committee work until October.

Final Days

As Sanford deteriorated physically, his vision for CLP seemed to intensify. He realized that instead of healing him, the Lord was probably going to take him to his eternal home. And although he was ready for that, he still wanted to do as much as he could to plan for the work of Christian publishing. He bore heavily the burden of the future. Would the work decline? Would there be others to carry on the vision? This was probably the most difficult part of his life to commit fully into the hands of the Lord.

Just a few days before Sanford died, his daughter Crystal wrote down what she understood him to say:

> Leave with the ministry my desire to leave a testimony that people be right with God and truly seek first His kingdom and righteousness. That when they face life's decisions they ask, "What will result in the most souls being saved and bring most glory to God?" and that they live holy lives.

That short message, though less articulate than in the days of his health, stands as an epitaph of his life.

On December 3 Sanford slipped into unconsciousness. In the evening, he rallied, and although he seemed conscious, there was very little communication. About 12:30 a.m. December 4, 1990, he passed away.

The February issue of CLE *LightLines* carried this report:

In Loving Memory

After suffering with cancer for several years, and especially the last few months, Brother Sanford, Founder and Director of Christian Light Publications, died peacefully in his sleep early Tuesday morning, December 4, at the age of 56 years and 21 days.

Thursday afternoon, December 6, a Memorial service was held at the Pike Mennonite Church, following a graveside service in the church cemetery. Taking part in the Memorial service were ministers from the Rawley Springs Mennonite Church (where Bro. Sanford served as pastor for 21 years), and others who had worked closely with Bro. Sanford at Christian Light. The service was planned as a time to worship God whom Bro. Sanford loved and served, and to challenge us who are left with the mission and concerns that were his special interests in life. . . .

His vision for God's will and confidence in God's blessing is concisely expressed in the CLE motto, printed on the cover of each CLE LIGHTUNIT, "God's truth equipping God's people to do God's work." . . .

Concerned that his vision was always in harmony with God's will, he had earlier this year invited interested individuals to share with him periodically in an evening of voluntary Bible study, fasting, and prayer.

Bro. Sanford believed that when we know God's will, we need to fulfill it. Many of us marvel at all he accomplished. Yet on his deathbed he lamented how little he had done. That feeling was partly due, no doubt, to the many projects he envisioned that remain for others to carry on to completion.

Bro. Sanford will be greatly missed, but we are confident that God has called him Home and that He will raise up others to go on with the unfinished work.

Miriam and Sterling Shank shortly before their marriage in 1985.

Another Death

When Sanford's son Sterling, who did typesetting for CLP, learned on his twenty-sixth birthday, January 9, 1990, that he had chronic kidney failure, he had two medical options: dialysis or transplant. Instead of either of those, he chose to trust the Lord for healing or for grace to bear the natural course of the illness.

One year later in March of 1991, Sterling and his wife Miriam (also a typesetter at CLP) learned through their own research that Sterling was in the final stages of kidney failure. Although they had known his condition was serious, they were struck by this sudden awareness. Two and one-half weeks later, on April 13, 1991, just four months after his father had died, Sterling passed away.

Sterling had taken graduate courses in Greek at a local college and was often consulted at CLP about original languages. Not until after he died did many realize how much of a Bible student he was. His Bible reading schedule called for as many as 15 chapters per day, as he read through the entire Bible once, and numerous parts repeatedly, each year.

They Died in Faith

Some no doubt questioned the decision of both Sanford and Sterling to trust the Lord for healing rather than take all medical procedures available. Few people know the untold hours of soul-searching, fasting, prayer, and counsel the Shanks went through in this matter: Should life be preserved at all cost? Is it presumptuous to simply trust one's case to the Lord? What is faith, and how does the Lord expect us to exercise it? How will He best be honored in situations of terminal illness?

Sanford and Sterling intended no claim to great faith. They intended no criticism of others who have made different decisions in similar situations. They simply both believed the Lord wanted them to trust Him, to find His grace for the things they needed to suffer, and to accept death when He chose to allow it.

A Special Testimony

"Sanford, I am not sure that I am qualified to do what you want me to do!"

"God's people can do God's work!" swiftly came his reply.

Such was my last conversation with Brother Sanford. I knew he was right, and yet my question seemed to persist. He was sick abed, and I was 3,000 miles away feeling fine. Why did he have more confidence in the Lord than I did? Well, that was Sanford. He had more courage and trust than I did—maybe more than most of us. . . .

Sanford was a man who was there when God needed him, and he was *ready, willing,* and *able.* Noah, Abraham, Moses, David, Jeremiah, Nehemiah, Paul, and Peter are all examples of godly men doing God's work. In such society, God's approval descends as showers of blessings on us all. . . .

Referring to Moses, God said, "My servant . . . is faithful in all mine house" (Numbers 12:7). This can be every believer's epitaph. It is a fitting conclusion for God's people who do God's work.

—Edward Gish

Part V: CLP Employees

The Lord gave the word: great was the company of those that published it (Psalm 68:11).

Dedication

One of the Lord's blessings to CLP has been staff members who have served faithfully, sometimes at considerable sacrifice. If you were to visit CLP during the evening or later in the night, you just might find someone busily working there. Some have worked long hours to meet a given schedule. Some have donated considerable time. During one period of economic recession, the group as a whole accepted a cut in wages in order that more funds might be available for ongoing operations. Some employees have loaned personal money to provide capital for specific needs. Probably all have worked at a lower wage than they could have earned for the same job performed in the industrial world.

Many employees have stayed through years of rapid growth when there were numerous changes, adjustments, and inconveniences.

Although most of CLP's regular employees have come from the Harrisonburg community, many have moved into the area from other states. A few employees do all or most of their work at their homes and are paid either on regular payroll or as self-employed individuals.

At the present time, employees come from thirteen states or provinces: Virginia, West Virginia, Wisconsin, Minnesota, Oregon, Texas, Idaho, North Dakota, Ohio, Pennsylvania, Florida, Illinois, and Nova Scotia. Employees from past years could add at least another twelve states and provinces: Indiana, Iowa, Missouri, Maryland, Michigan, Georgia, Kansas, Mississippi, California, Ontario, Manitoba, and Alberta.

John Hartzler, General Manager, in his present office located upstairs in Building No. 1.

A complete list of employees is given in Appendix A, but the following have made significant contributions to CLP in their ten years or more of service. (A few of them were largely on Park View Press payroll, but helped considerably with CLP work.)

Ruth Alger (1981-present): Works in layout.

Susan Heatwole Anderson (1973-1993): Worked in typesetting both in the office and at her home.

Roger Berry (1972-present): Wrote two social studies textbooks; has written Sunday school curriculum including a special quarter on nonconformity; edited *Companions* since 1983.

Aldine (1957-1985) and Sallie Brenneman (1957-present): Father and mother of Merna Shank, helped significantly with the use of their buildings and property and donated much time—Aldine in helping with such things as payroll and maintenance, Sallie in office-related and miscellaneous hand operations.

Betty Brenneman (1969-present): Has served in darkroom and stripping as well as proofreading and bindery work.

Living next door to CLP, Aldine and Sallie Brenneman not only helped with regular work, but were also available at odd times for odd jobs.

Ruth Alger, whose main work is layout, also helps in other areas. Here she is collating signatures of Into All the World *for the fourth grade social studies textbook.*

David Burkholder (1962-1977): Shop foreman supervising PVP and CLP operations; edited *Companions* 1973-1983.

John Coblentz (1979-present): Author of the *Christian Family Living* series and several other CLP books; has written Sunday school curriculum including a special quarter on nonresistance; editor of *Just for You*; works from his home in Ohio (formerly Minnesota) as editor and as writer of original CLE curriculum.

Doris Greider (1976-1988): Specialized in computer operations.

Hilda Harlow (1977-present): Housekeeping and proofreading. Hilda has won a special spot in employees' hearts in recent years as manager of the ten o'clock popcorn center.

Lloyd Hartzler (1971-present): Office editor; Lloyd has served on numerous committees as well as the CLP Board.

John Hartzler (1971-present): Lloyd's son; John has served as General Manager of CLP since 1979. His work load is immense and includes general oversight of operations, manager of personnel, treasurer, and Board member. In 1980 John learned he had a malignancy in his thyroid. Through many prayers, an operation, treatment, and thyroid medication, John's problem has been corrected. The people at CLP continue to give thanks for John's health—and for the countless ways he serves them as General Manager.

Mildred Martin (1964-1976): Typist and layout person; Mildred worked primarily for PVP, but was co-editor of *Story Mates* and *Partners* for a number of years.

Fred Miller (1981-present): Does editorial work from his home in West Virginia; directs the Book and Tract Committee, CLE teacher training, and fall workshops.

Boyd and Margaret Shank (Sanford's parents), who encouraged the work of CLP and assisted in various ways.

Pete Peters spent one year at the CLP headquarters and has continued a variety of CLE related assignments from his home in Canada.

Pete Peters (1983-present): Spent a year at CLP in writing and editing; now works from his home in Alberta. Pete frequently helps with the CLE fall workshop tours.

Paul Reed (1979-present): Began by supervising the revision of AOP science materials; he now directs the CLE General Office and with his wife Ethel manages the homeschool division of CLE. Paul also serves as editor of *LightLines*, the CLE newsletter.

Boyd (1957-1980) and Margaret Shank (1957-present): Sanford's parents, contributed much by their encouraging counsel and personal involvement—Boyd running a press and working in layout, Margaret in voluntarily cooking meals for training sessions and helping with mailings, etc.

Carol Shank (1974-present): Serves as secretary to the General Manager and makes arrangement for permissions to use copyrighted material.

Crystal Shank (1979-present): Daughter of Sanford and Merna Shank; Crystal is in charge of bookkeeping and serves as editor of *Partners*.

Miriam Shank —wife of Sterling (1982-present): Daughter-in-law of Sanford and Merna Shank; Miriam works in typesetting and is editor of *Story Mates*.

Zela Shenk (1967-present): Works in mailing room and bindery (was recently on temporary leave for several months, caring for her one-hundred-seven-year-old mother.)

Lula Showalter (1976-present): Worked for years in the PVP office; now schedules jobs and works in layout and bindery.

Mary Catherine Showalter (1969-present): Mary Catherine was in charge of bookkeeping for years, but because of the poor health of her parents she needed to discontinue. After being off for about a year, she is now working part-time.

Eva Sonifrank Glanzer (1978-present): Works in typesetting.

John Swartz (1979-present): Supervised revision of AOP curriculum; continues to give oversight to development of CLE curriculum materials.

Merna Shank, Secretary, at her desk in the one office which has not changed size or location.

Merna Shank—Sanford's wife—has served from the beginning and has contributed immensely to the work of CLP. Merna serves as Board secretary and promotions secretary besides carrying out many other secretarial duties. She also serves as editor of *Alight* and *imPRESSions* and heads the in-house "Sunshine Committee."

Merna is the one to ask when a Board member wonders what was decided "way back when," the one to write a poem when one is needed on the spot, the one who can take a phone dictation by shorthand on a rushed article or ad, the one to edit a transcribed sermon so the sentences and paragraphs are properly arranged, the one to write an announcement for employees, one who will listen and offer wise counsel to a troubled sister employee. . . . If you need information, and no one else knows where to find it, check with Merna.

In the work at CLP, Merna's discreet, unobtrusive manner has been as priceless as the contribution of her skills.

From an Employee

In the fall of 1974 I ventured 3,000 miles to start a job at CLP. That was a long way for this home girl but my courage was bolstered with the company of a friend from home making the move with me and the fact that I was just going to stay six months.

My work at CLP has varied over the last 19 years (I haven't gotten around to leaving yet), but it presently includes being secretary to the General Manager as well as securing permission to include non-CLP material in our publications.

I have been richly blessed to be able to be involved in a Christian work like this. To be working together with a team of other Christians meeting needs of people on their way to eternity is a very rewarding place to be.

It has been strengthening to my faith in God to see ways He has directed and supplied needs here at CLP that were beyond human planning. One example of that which stands out to me was His sending help to us over the time of building the new building and moving into it. There were several key persons who volunteered in that work and filled unique places with amazing abilities. Their availability and service leave lasting impressions on me of God's provision and care.

Other times of His supplying special financial needs in unusual ways have been meaningful assurances to me personally that our God is alive.

His direction in the CLE curriculum and ways He is using it in touching lives is a demonstration of His work and power that speaks loudly to me. In fact, probably the biggest reward He has given me in my years here is hearing of those whose lives He is changing, using as one of His tools printed material He has directed us to produce.

—Carol Shank

Carol Shank, Secretary to the General Manager, is also Permissions Secretary and handles numerous contacts with other publishers.

Voluntary Service

Voluntary service has been of major significance in CLP's history, and it is impossible to know or have record of everybody who has contributed in this way. Some VS workers have received a VS allowance on a regular payroll basis. Some have donated all their services and provided their own housing without any remuneration from CLP. Repeatedly, VS workers have come to help with given projects—an evening or a day, a week or two, a couple of months, a year or more.

Although CLP does not presently maintain an established VS unit with long-term houseparents, VS workers are a normal part of the workforce. Over the years CLP has rented three different houses for varying lengths of time, some of which have provided a place for VS workers. Several apartments and houses conveniently close to CLP have also been available not only for VS workers, but also for other employees.

Probably every kind of work done at CLP has at some time been carried out by VS workers. This includes not only workers in maintenance, bindery, mailing, and press operation, but also office workers, writers, editors, and administrators. This donation of labor has been of immeasurable worth to the publication of Christian literature.

Of no less importance is the voluntary service of GIVING performed by hundreds of the CLP constituency from their homes.

The house at 1145 Woodleigh Court where numerous VS girls lived and where CLE training sessions were held from 1980 through 1990.

David Heatwole working on one of many small construction projects that he has completed for various offices.

Only the Lord has an accurate record of all the voluntary service rendered to Him, for He it is who stirs the hearts of the willing. Surely He who notices even a cup of cold water in His name will not let any service go unrewarded.

From an Employee

"O LORD, I know that the way of man is not in himself: it is not in man that walketh to direct his steps" (Jeremiah 10:23). We have almost completed our one-year term of VS and have enjoyed the place and the people the Lord has directed us to. We will miss each one but are looking forward to going "home" to Manitoba and seeing our families again.

Myrna has been working in the computer room, processing CLE orders, etc. Gerry has been involved in many areas of work—maintenance, carpentry, and later in mail pick-up and delivery and also operating one of the presses.

We've appreciated the daily morning devotions at CLP before we begin the day's work. From our experience here we've learned that the work here involves a lot more than first expected. May the Lord keep prospering it.

—Gerry and Myrna Reimer

Irene Stauffer at work in the first CLE mailing room in Building No. 1.

— *From an Employee* —————————————————

One impression from working here has been the marvel of the human voice which makes each person unique. A gamut of scale and range of tone provides variety and establishes identity of the youngest to the "semi-senior" and senior citizens. How this conglomerate of voices can be steered away from discord and chaos and funneled into a blend of harmonious singing during devotions is a wonder of creation! "O Lord, forgive me when I whine,/ I have two ears, The world is mine."

The thought from the Westminster Chimes is wished for all: "Lord, through this hour,/ Be Thou our guide,/ So, by Thy power,/ No foot shall slide."

—Hettie Showalter

Keeping in Touch

CLP administrators have for many years met with employees each morning for ten or fifteen minutes for song, prayer, and announcements. In this time, employees have sung through several hymnbooks. They also have prayed together over countless personal concerns and needs for themselves, their families, friends, and users of CLP materials.

Another relational tie has been *imPRESSions*, a weekly news sheet prepared for employees each Friday. Employees are invited to contribute items of interest about themselves, their work, their associates, or any other subject of general interest. Submissions include answers to prayer, choice excerpts from private reading, reminders of right and wrong English usage, instructions on job performance, as well as occasional touches of humor.

Following are a few examples of inspirational entries in *imPRESSions*:

"Calvary is God's blood bank for a sick world."

"People who are always wanting what they don't have are always getting what they didn't want."

A clergyman in England asked a dying Christian woman where she found the Saviour, and she gave him a piece of paper torn from an American journal containing part of one of C. H. Spurgeon's sermons. The scrap had been wrapped around a package that came to her from Australia. The words of Spurgeon were read by her and were the means of leading her to Christ. Commenting on this incident, a writer says, "Think of it: a sermon preached in England, printed in America, in some way coming to Australia, a part of it used as wrapping paper there, coming back to England, was the means of converting this woman!"

The more you do, the more will be asked of you.
    That is the blessed penalty for willingness.
The more you do, the more you will be able to do.
    That is the blessed law of effort.
The more you do, the more it will mean to you.
    That is the blessed reward in the Master's service.
They know Him best who serve Him most.
                —Joseph Murrey

Efficiency Motto: Mistakes never made need never be corrected.

Employee families enjoy a picnic supper along the river at Oren Heatwoles in 1972.

Mary Beth Bentz at work in the shipping department.

Not only has CLP tried to maintain the spirit of family closeness, but some employees have indeed been family in the literal sense. Numerous husband-wife teams have served at CLP together, and quite a few times there have been second and third generation employees, either working simultaneously or some years apart. So, although the fifty-plus employees are not mostly from any one family tree, they have included husbands, wives, sisters, brothers, grandparents, grandchildren, parents, children, uncles, aunts, nephews, nieces, and cousins.

Jerry Bentz, Mailing Supervisor, preparing "Just for You" for shipping. Metal trays stacked in the background hold the folded papers as they leave the bindery. After mailing is completed, remaining stock will be boxed for the warehouse.

Employees at Work

Richard E. Shank, of Hagerstown, Maryland, on the Board of Directors since 1982 and President since 1990, assisted in the management of production operations 1980-81.

Sterling Beachy, Shop Foreman, contemplates questions of quality control as newly printed sheets come off the press.

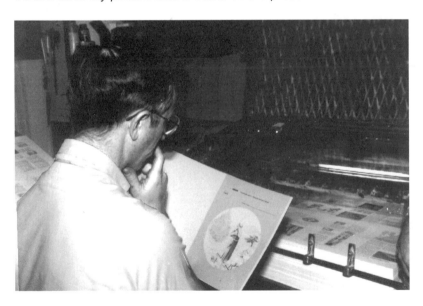

Elam Heatwole, who supervises maintenance and is in charge of purchasing, works in his office located upstairs in Building No. 1 in part of what was formerly the darkroom.

Karen Knicely working at the web press. Four-hundred-pound rolls of paper are placed at one end of the press, run through in a continuous strip, and automatically cut into 11 x 17 inch printed sheets at the other end. One run through the press will print both sides of the sheet in two colors or one side in four colors.

James T. Shank assembling sample packets to be distributed at homeschool conventions and sent to those requesting them.

John Hartzler (right) and his wife Ruby serving ice cream to the construction crew working on Building No. 2 one hot afternoon in August, 1991.

Roy Strubhar packages orders for items from the general catalog other than Sunday school and CLE curriculum materials.

Jean (Hartman) Martin, hand collating extra signatures required at the Macey.

Donna Plank (above) pulls orders and helps package CLE and Sunday school materials.

Jose Liscano making adjustments at the Macey collator.

Jerry Bentz using the stock-picker to place or remove inventory from top-level warehouse shelves in Building No. 2.

Angie Cash working in CLE's computer order department.

Julia Rhodes and Lula Showalter collating hardcover textbook signatures from the revolving round table.

Beginnings of the snack store for employees at break time. Kevin, Crystal, and Sterling Shank "managed" this store in 1969.

David
Hartzler's
duties in the
Mailing
Department
include
morning and
afternoon
mail runs to
the post
office in
Harrisonburg.

Layman Apartments next door to CLP, home to numerous CLP VSers.

View of the computer room after it was moved upstairs, but before the completion of renovation which divided operations and desks into several rooms. Wesley Burkholder (foreground), Beth (Martin) Knicely, Angie Cash, and Sue Byler.

Just one of those days!

Miriam I. Martin, full-time staff artist from 1979-1988.

Andy Korver (right) at the Macey Collator.

Below: Tim Anderson (facing camera) and Tim Korver operating the Didde Web press in the new pressroom. 1981

107

George and Verna Cross served in VS almost two years and were involved in assorted activities. George (above) enjoyed outdoor maintenance, and here with the help of employees Karen Knicely, Carol Shank, and Sterling Beachy, he proved he knew how to get the "kinks" out of a non-paved driveway.

Verna (below) helped in various cooking and office-related jobs as well as in the bindery. Here she is using the plastic wrap machine.

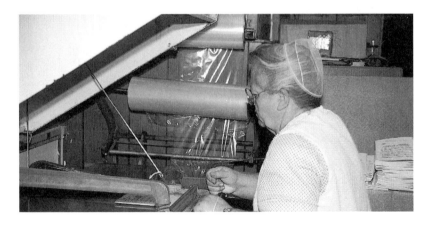

Right: One of PVP/CLP's "accessories" 1966 to 1985. The cat appears to be checking the clock to see how soon office hours will begin. He early learned how to be the first one inside when the door opened.

Below: Buried treasure at CLP's front door, March 1994. The employee who owned this car had other means of transportation home.

109

Employee Group, November 1992

On steps: Kathryn (Knicely) Good, Sonia (Burkholder) Knicely,
Miriam Martin, Treda Layman, Naomi Myers, Eva Glanzer,
Esther Heatwole, Elizabeth Hostetter, Bonnie (Martin) Good,
Zela Shenk, Sue Byler, Earl Martin, Steve Zimmerman,
Sterling Beachy.
On ground, all rows together left to right: Joanna Rohrer, Frieda
Thiessen, Karen Knicely, Lula Showalter, Angie Cash, Julia
Rhodes, Crystal Shank, Donna Plank, Bethany Hartzler, Mary
Alice McDorman, Rosalyn Strubhar, Carol Shank, Mary Martin,
Betty Brenneman, Ethel Reed, Ruth Alger, Hilda Harlow,
Merna Shank, Kevin Shank, John Hartzler, Elam Heatwole.
In doorway, first row: Roger Berry, Paul Reed, Melvin Thiessen,
John Thiessen, Robert Wilson
second row: Lloyd Hartzler, Jerry Bentz, Jose Liscano,
Wesley Burkholder, James Hershberger.
back row: Roy Strubhar, Charles Hoff, David Miller,
Norman Yoder.

Hilda Harlow popping corn for employees' 10 a.m. break.

From an Employee

I began working at CLP (then Park View Press) in November 1977. Prior to that I had cared for many children while their parents worked. After twenty years of tending other peoples' children and with my own two now grown, I thought I would like several days a week of work at the press.

I told Sanford I would be willing to do anything— maybe cleaning. The second week I was there Sanford told me he would like me to help proofread the next day. That sounded very good since I dearly love to read.

I work there now two days a week. In the mornings I do light housekeeping. At ten o'clock break I am pretty popular because at that time I pop corn. Many of my co-workers partake of it. I think I have them spoiled.

When the school curriculum was first started, Mary Brubaker and I pulled orders. A checker checked them. I did that for a couple of years. Now I keep busy cleaning and proofreading. I get plenty of exercise in the mornings, and after lunch I read to my proofreading partner, Naomi Myers.

I really enjoy that, and some material is so interesting that I feel a little guilty to take pay. Sometimes we find mistakes that are funny. Like the other week something read, "We need more faithful worriers." I told Naomi my faithful worrying wasn't in vain after all! It was meant to read, however, "We need more faithful warriors."

111

I'm sure the Lord helped me get my job at CLP. As soon as I started working here, I found everyone so kind to me and to each other. One of the things that impresses me most is meeting together at 8 a.m. for devotions. We sing several beautiful hymns, read the Bible, and have prayer requests. We pray for the work, the workers, for the people who receive the wonderful Christian material, and anything on our minds.

I have many good friends here, both young and old, and I would rather work here than anywhere else.

May God continue to bless Christian Light Publications.

—Hilda Harlow

Current Committees

Over the years many internal committees have served in the organization. Here are listed the current committees with a brief description of their work. In each committee, the chairman is listed first.

Board of Directors

Members: Leon Yoder, Lloyd Hartzler, Richard Shank, John Hartzler, Glenn Martin, Mark Heatwole, David G. Martin, associate member.

The Board of Directors has responsibility for the overall operation of CLP. Monthly meetings include setting policies, giving guidance to the General Manager, and planning for the future.

Executive Committee

Members: Richard Shank, Leon Yoder, John Hartzler

The Executive Committee meets more often than the CLP Board for consultation in the actual carrying out of the Board's directives.

Finance Committee

Members: Richard Shank, John Hartzler, Leon Yoder

Responsibilities of this Committee include reviewing the financial situation regularly, projecting income and expense, preparing budgets, giving financial frameworks to persons or committees working on projects, studying financial trends, and bringing recommendations to the Board as to how needs should be met.

CLE Committee

Members: John Swartz, Pete Peters, Leon Yoder, Robert Wilson

This Committee has general oversight of the CLE program, arranging for curriculum development and establishing policies and procedures. They try to keep abreast of needs and trends and make plans and recommendations accordingly.

Production Committee

Members: John Hartzler, Elam Heatwole, Kevin Shank

Originally set up to work through specific personnel problems, this Committee now serves as an internal counseling group for the General Manager on day-to-day business.

Book Review Committee

Members: John Swartz, Roger Berry, Chester Martin

CLP retails many books it does not publish. When a book is recommended to CLP, the Book Review Committee is responsible to review the book, give it a rating according to established guidelines, and decide whether or not CLP should handle the book.

The CLE Committee in session. Left to right: Pete Peters; John Swartz, Chairman; Leon Yoder; Robert Wilson.

Bible School Committee

Members: Lloyd Hartzler, John Hartzler, Glenn Heatwole

Initially the Bible School Committee was established to plan the Bible School curriculum and work with writers, reviewers, and editors. Today, this Committee is responsible to plan for revision as necessary and is also responsible to arrange for a new adult study each year.

Sunday School

Members: John Hartzler, Roger Berry, James Zehr, Leon Yoder

The Sunday School Committee plans the Sunday school materials (usually based on the International Sunday School Lessons) and arranges for writers. This Committee also makes recommendations to the CLP Board for new writers, artists, and editors as necessary. Members keep alert to comments from users of the Sunday school materials and pass on suggestions to the CLP Board as well as to writers and editors.

The Production Committee discusses day-to-day operations. Left to right: John Hartzler, General Manager; Kevin Shank; Elam Heatwole.

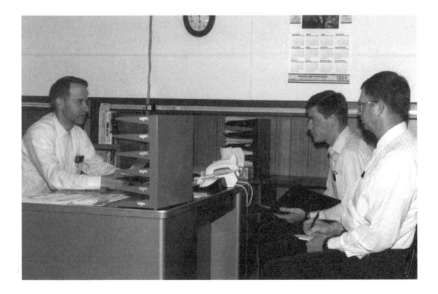

Fred Miller, Director of CLE field services and teacher training and Chairman of the Book and Tract Committee, does much work at his home in West Virginia. The Book and Tract Committee members, living in four different communities, often carry on their work through 6 a.m. telephone committee meetings.

Book and Tract Committee
Members: Fred Miller, Leon Yoder, Lloyd Hartzler, John Coblentz
Members of the Book and Tract Committee review manuscripts submitted for publication and then meet regularly in telephone conferences to discuss editorial work and publishing. This Committee also plans publishing projects (such as the *Christian Family Living* Series).

Newsletter Planning Committee
Members: John Hartzler, Lloyd Hartzler, Mark Heatwole, Merna Shank
For each newsletter, this Committee has a planning session, pooling ideas of each member and planning what items to include. The chairman then assigns these projects to writers, later collects them, and gives guidance to layout and composition.

Alight Committee

Members: Leon Yoder, Elam and Ellen Heatwole, Merna Shank

Committee members share ideas and suggestions, but the editor has the main responsibility for each issue of *Alight. Alight* is published bi-monthly, and its aim demonstrates the missionary vision of CLP—"to share what the Lord is doing in lives and to promote interest in being about the Father's business."

Spanish Committee

Members: Glenn Martin, Leon Yoder, John Swartz

The Spanish Committee was appointed in 1990 to work with brethren in Costa Rica who were interested in Spanish school curriculum. This Committee continues to work on the development of Spanish materials, and directs the translation of existing literature (such as issues of *Just for You*) into Spanish.

Extension Committee

Members: Lloyd Hartzler, Fred Miller, Glenn Martin

The Extension Committee was set up in 1988 to respond to growing requests from readers seeking further spiritual help and fellowship in a faithful church. This Committee continues to be challenged with helping seekers become part of a church that will meet their needs. (Most inquiries are from users of CLE materials.)

Testimonies From CLP Board Members

It is difficult to appreciate fully any organization when your knowledge is limited to what you see. That was the situation for most of us when we were first elected as a member of the Christian Light Board.

The complexity of giving oversight and leadership to a nonprofit organization composed of many departments, while supplying a large variety of literature to diverse customers is an enlightening experience. Personnel, finances, production, and administration are interrelated, and each have their continual tests and trials. But the Lord has been faithful, and on days when there was no apparent solution to a problem, the Lord always graciously supplied the needed direction.

The encouragement and enthusiasm of faithful brethren

throughout the States and Canada has been a highlight in the work at Christian Light. Like new Board members, they have risen to the challenge as they learned where and how they could lend assistance.

We rejoice that our financial situation is no longer precarious, although concerted, continuing effort is required to meet our obligations and provide funds for new projects. It is with confidence that we face the future. The Lord has provided brethren for the Board who have a range of skills and abilities. The Board's ability to "press forward for the work in Christ Jesus" is enhanced by a harmonious working relationship. May the Lord continue to bless the work at Christian Light to increase His kingdom here on earth.

—Richard Shank

One of the blessings we learn in Christian experience is the contribution others can make. When each one is committed to the total cause and submitted to Christ, the individual gifts blend into a unity and oneness.

While the work of CLP combines the efforts of many individuals, the goal is to exalt Christ and help more people to know Him. Another purpose is to help those who are believers to grow in faith by use of the literature produced.

I am grateful for the opportunity to serve with the CLP team in this literature ministry. May our vision be clear.

—Glenn E. Martin

Over the years being involved in a number of different operations has been educational and interesting. This has given me a view of what it takes to develop an article or book and make it available to meet various needs in the world.

It is always interesting to hear from others who have read the material and appreciate it and want more. This helps us see the deep need and the challenge CLP has in trying to meet the need in whatever way we can.

I also appreciate how it takes many people committed to God to continue with the work of spreading the Gospel. Without the faithful financial support of the many who read and use CLP's material, the CLP staff would indeed have a difficult, if not impossible, task in continuing. May we continue serving Him faithfully.

—Mark N. Heatwole

If someone had told me 30 years ago that I would spend 20-some years at a job behind a desk, I would have questioned how well he knew me. But that is where God has placed me since I started working for CLP in 1971.

My work as office editor has been challenging and rewarding. (Isn't that the way it is with any service for the Lord?) How careful we need to be to publish only that which is in harmony with God's Word! I have enjoyed digging into the Word to check doctrines, to search out details, and to note accurately what a passage says.

One thing that has especially impressed me in this work is how human we are. No matter how careful writers, editors, typesetters, and proofreaders try to be, mistakes still have a way of sneaking through at times.

A second thing I have appreciated in working here at CLP is the value of teamwork. Whether it is finding errors or discerning truth, teamwork is a real blessing. I have enjoyed consulting with my brethren, getting a broader counsel on many issues that have come across my desk.

One of the biggest blessings and perhaps the greatest challenge in my work has been with our Extension Committee in recent years.

Board of Directors 1994.

Left to right: Glenn Martin; Mark Heatwole; Lloyd Hartzler; Leon Yoder, Chairman; John Hartzler; Richard Shank.

118

Many people across our country who are using materials published by CLP, particularly our school curriculum, are accepting the Word and are looking for a more Biblical fellowship. Helping honest seekers, whether by letter or by phone, has been a joyful challenge to my life and has been another confirmation of my need for wisdom from above.

Praise the Lord for the many people who are yet seeking the way of true discipleship!

—Lloyd Hartzler

When our Lord chose men to carry on His work, many of them were the common laborers of His day. A few may have been educated, but some were "ignorant and unlearned" fishermen. But what counts most is not the "polish" on the tool, but the power and skill of the Master along with the availability of the tool. I suppose this truth has impressed me more than any other during my years with the work at CLP.

This truth has been evident on a company level. In many ways the Lord has blessed beyond what man could do. For example, in spite of predictions that Mennonites cannot produce a satisfactory school curriculum, yet when God's people give themselves in obedience to His promptings, it can be done.

I have also thrilled at the evidence of this truth in individuals. We have been grateful for some who have brought their acquired skills to the organization, but many have come quite "ignorant and unlearned," inexperienced, and imperfect. Very few had any knowledge or experience in education, printing, or publishing, and yet as they continue to give themselves to the service of the Master, He can accomplish His purposes—at times, perhaps, in spite of the "tools."

I feel the Lord led me to CLP. I was a young farm boy, had much to learn, and have many times felt very inadequate for the task. My desire is simply to be where the Lord wants me to be, and to serve Him with my best as He gives me grace. My prayer for CLP is that it might continue to be a lighthouse to those who are seeking the way, an encouragement to those who are in the way, and an example of what the Lord can do through those who give themselves to His work.

—John Hartzler

Looking to the Future

Our vision at Christian Light Publications is twofold. First, the world is lost, and opportunities for sharing the Gospel are all about us. Whether it's from door to door, in prisons, on the street, at our work, or in the grocery store, Christians are to be ambassadors.

CLP aims to provide attractive, easy to understand, and thought-provoking literature that can help God's people reach out with the Gospel message. We plan for our growing list of tracts to grow longer. Timely subjects need to be spoken to. We must proclaim the light of truth that points the way to hope and peace in a darkening world.

The second area of our work is a ministry to the church, providing material that brightens the pilgrim's path toward clearer knowledge of God and His will. Parents are looking for direction as they guide their children through disturbing times. Church leaders appreciate material that strengthens conviction. Christians young and old benefit from honest and clear Bible teaching that helps them be better servants for God.

The CLE school curriculum has been an inspiration to many students and parents. It needs revision and improvement to be even more effective. We want to help develop and publish more Christian school material in Spanish. Books and pamphlets need to be published that address crucial issues facing our homes and churches. Courses and lessons must continue to be developed for Bible schools and Sunday schools.

We must proclaim the light of truth that builds and strengthens the faithful brotherhood in times of increasing religious confusion and apostasy. We must remind one another of the comforting words of hope—Christ is returning for His own; be comforted and strengthened; be watchful; be faithful.

As the future marches toward us, these areas of need will grow increasingly critical as Satan's power increases among a decadent society and an apostate church. We have a responsibility to the lost and to those found in Christ. Proclaiming God's truth is the answer for both.

—Leon Yoder

Part VI: CLP Today

Let thy work appear unto thy servants, and thy glory unto their children. And let the beauty of the LORD our God be upon us: and establish thou the work of our hands upon us; yea, the work of our hands establish thou it (Psalm 90:16, 17).

Reorganization

The passing of Sanford Shank in December of 1990 called for rethinking the organizational structure of CLP. Although John Hartzler had served as General Manager of CLP since 1979, Sanford had served as Director. The vision and the oversight had rested largely upon him.

The Board realized, especially through the last half of 1990, that changes would need to be made. In the reorganization that followed in 1991, Leon Yoder was asked to serve as Chairman of the Board of Directors. Board member Richard Shank was named President of CLP. John Hartzler continued to serve as General Manager, and he was also asked to serve on the Board of Directors. Under those organizational leaders are many committees, some with overlapping personnel, but each with a particular work to do.

At present, Paul Reed continues to head the homeschool division and serves as editor of *LightLines*; John Swartz, from West Virginia, is chairman of the CLE Committee responsible for curriculum planning and development. Fred Miller, likewise from West Virginia, is in charge of training and workshops. He also chairs the Book and Tract Committee. Lloyd Hartzler is Office Editor and chairman of the Bible School and Extension Committees. Kevin Shank (Sanford and Merna's son) heads the Art Department, and serves as Safety Director. Wesley Burkholder is responsible for computer operations. Norman Yoder (son of Leon Yoder) is in charge of composition. Sterling Beachy is foreman in production. Jerry Bentz is the mailing supervisor. Elam Heatwole has charge of purchasing, housekeeping, and maintenance. Lula Showalter is responsible for scheduling. Crystal Shank oversees the bookkeeping. And Mark Bear, from his home in Idaho, continues to arrange CLE curriculum exhibits at homeschool conventions.

As Sanford stressed many times, CLP works best when there is *teamwork*. That concept is as necessary today as it ever was in CLP's history. No one person does the work alone; each one, however much in the background he may be, has his necessary role to fill.

Special Publications

Over the years, CLP has published various books and tracts that have stood out not only in sales, but also in effect. The scope and volume of the CLE curriculum give it a prominence that sometimes overshadows these publishing projects. Here are the stories of some of the tracts and books that are currently available from CLP.

Wesley Burkholder, as Supervisor of Computer Operations and Order Department, gives direction to daily computer operations. His work also includes helping to determine and carry out sales policies.

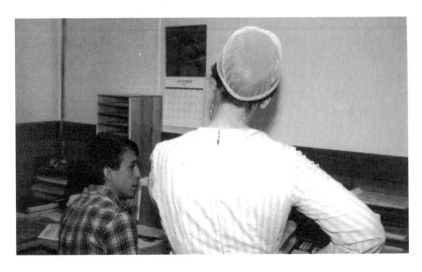

Supervisor Norman Yoder oversees the operations of the Prepress Department. CLP has been using Macintosh computers for typesetting since 1991.

The tract *The Significance of the Christian Woman's Veiling,* by Merle Ruth, has borne fruit among Mennonites and non-Mennonites, in the United States and in foreign countries. After reading this tract and studying the Scriptures, a man from California wrote, "We would like to know if my wife can order any of your woman's headcoverings from you, and if so, at what price. If not, where then? We would appreciate your help."

A woman from Nigeria had these interesting comments:

> I fellowship with the Deeper Christian Life Ministry and I am also a worker in the Lord's vineyard. In my fellowship the women veil their head all day long and it is thought commonly amongst other Christians that it is a Deeper Christian Life Ministry (DCLM) doctrine. I was exceedingly glad to read it that I made so many photocopies and sent out to some sisters.

The tract *Calvinism/Arminianism, Which?* by Roger Berry, has likewise produced significant responses. One man who has for 54 years been a member of a denomination that teaches Calvinism wrote requesting copies of this tract. He said, "I have never accepted unconditional security."

An investigative team visiting the Dominican Republic gave this report:

> We were very encouraged as we traveled from church to church, visiting with Dominican pastors and discovering a common yearning for a more Scriptural fellowship, doctrinal teaching and stability. The pastors we visited with were dedicated and studious.
>
> The present openness towards us is in part a backlash to the introduction of Calvinism into their conference by American missionaries. . . . It appears that the greater part of the native ministry was prompt and thorough in their renunciation of this heresy, and soon broke with the conference, taking with them the bulk of native churches.
>
> Somewhere along the way they came in contact with the Spanish translation of *Calvinism-Arminianism, Which?* We received a request for 5,000 of these tracts which we forwarded to CLP. This tract must have been thoroughly distributed among those churches. Everywhere we went it was known and everyone we talked to appreciated it and was thoroughly convinced of the error of Calvinism.

In 1979, CLP published a children's storybook entitled *Storytime With Grandma.* The stories were compiled by Mary Elizabeth Yoder from several older books long out of print. The first printing of 10,500 soon sold out. The next year 15,000 copies were printed, and in 1981 another 15,000. In 1991 the fourth printing of 10,000 was issued. In an age when millions of children are being given the emotional, mental, and spiritual junk food of cartoons and monsters via TV and video, it is thrilling to realize that some children are having the nourishing experience of wholesome stories being read to them.

In 1984, Elizabeth Lapp, who had personally experienced the anguish of divorce, wrote *Journal of Tears.* The author focused not on the lurid narrative but on the feelings, the practical struggles, the day-by-day search for the will of God, and the insights He graciously gave her. The first printing of 5,000 copies sold rapidly, and in 1985 another 10,000 were printed.

In 1986, in a joint venture with Calvary Publications, CLP printed 10,000 copies of a small book entitled *Music in Biblical Perspective* by John Coblentz. This booklet, now in its second printing, has been used with an accompanying study guide by many churches in group study. One person who ordered 20 copies wrote:

> It is the best written and most intelligent writing to my knowledge that I have seen. And the author manages to keep a level head and not just lapse into ranting and raving about the evils of music and instruments. . . . I would like to see more of the same type of writing on current subjects.

In 1989, a fictional book by Romaine Stauffer entitled *Circle of Love* depicted the temptations and struggles many young men faced in the IW program in the 1960s. The book also revealed the weaknesses of the Mennonite church community in not meeting the spiritual needs of many of those young men. Now in its second printing, this book continues its message to readers that avoiding the military is not enough, that nothing will substitute for solid, Biblical conviction.

In 1990, missionary wife Nancy Stutzman compiled a book of devotional meditations for women, entitled *Tea Leaves*. The book is now in its second printing. The feeling of many women is well-stated by this woman from Ontario:

> A friend of mine gave me a copy of your devotional book, *Tea Leaves*, for Christmas. This book came into my life exactly where and when I most needed it, and I wanted to thank you as well as my friend. . . .
> Last fall we moved to an isolated Indian reserve, which was a new experience for us. My husband is teaching at a Christian school and I am busy at home with three children, aged 4, 2, and 7 months. It has been wonderful to sample a "cup of tea" and find out to my surprise and enormous

comfort that I am not the first woman to have gone through these experiences.

CLP's fastest selling book has been *Awaiting the Dawn*, by Dorcas Hoover. This book relates the true account of the martyrdom of John Troyer in the mountains of Guatemala and the trauma and grief of his wife and five children as they pulled their lives together after his death. The first printing of 6,500 came out early in 1992. In six months it was sold out. The second printing of 11,000 also sold well . . . and continues to sell, as testimony to the power of a life given for the Lord.

Also in 1992, Christian Light produced the book *Christian Family Living*, by John Coblentz. This was the first in a series that includes:
God's Will for My Body—Guidance for Adolescents
God's Will for Love in Marriage—Cultivating Marital Intimacy
What the Bible Says About Marriage, Divorce, and Remarriage
Two chapters in the book *Christian Family Living* were printed as separate booklets (the chapter on singlehood and the chapter on

John Coblentz, staff writer, editor, and member of the Book and Tract Committee, works from his home in Ohio (formerly Minnesota). John's books include the Christian Family Living *series and others.*

dating). The following response expresses the thoughts of many regarding this series:

> My husband and I have been so enriched by *Christian Family Living*, by John Coblentz. I have never come across such a practical book on the actual living out of the Christian life. . . . I praise God that he took the time and effort to share this with us in book form.

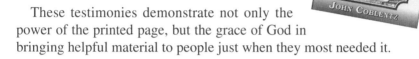

These testimonies demonstrate not only the power of the printed page, but the grace of God in bringing helpful material to people just when they most needed it.

Original Curriculum

"Behold, the fear of the LORD, that is wisdom; and to depart from evil is understanding" (Job 28:28). At the heart of Christian Light's

Robert Wilson, member of the CLE Committee, assists in CLE curriculum revision and development.

plan for future curriculum is the desire to present all subjects from a perspective that fully honors the Lord.

Planning is underway for an original CLE elementary math curriculum. Yes, even math reflects a world view, more than most people realize. Instead of exercises that compute how far to the fair or how much for the movie, God's people desire exercises that deal with how far to the annual meeting, how much for missions, and how the principles of stewardship apply in the handling of finances.

Perspectives of Truth in Literature, a high school literature course, approaches the study of literature from a godly viewpoint. A second high school literature course in the same series, *Perspectives of Life in Literature*, is projected to be available soon. Language Arts 1100 has been replaced. The new course has an emphasis on writing skills along with a study of U.S. and Canadian literature. This makes three original CLE high school courses in the language arts.

A reader series for the elementary grades is also in the planning stage. This series is to be designed for use in classroom schools, individualized schools, and homeschools. The new series is planned to be an integral part of CLE's own elementary language arts program.

From an Employee

I began working for Park View Press even before Building No. 1 existed. In the basement of our home I helped collate some of the first books printed, when collating was one hundred percent a manual operation, and some jobs involved miles of walking around tables picking up the different sections.

For many collating jobs now, today's efficient machine requiring only one operator, has little suction cups that can pick up as many as seventeen different sections at the same time, placing them on stacks which are automatically moved to the next station where another section is added. At the end of the line the collated material is automatically stitched, folded, and trimmed.

All these years of growth and change have brought many different people and experiences into the lives of those associated with the work. I value the association and fellowship I experienced with everybody whose life touched mine. And I trust that my life may have reflected to them also the sunshine of God's love.

Some customers who came into the office were more pleasant than others, but all of them left an influence of some kind. I think of the morning we were blessed with a gentle soaking rain—just what our dry ground needed and the perfect answer for which many people had been praying. In response to my "Good morning," one caller replied gruffly, "I don't see anything good about it." Such customers were a reminder to thank God for His daily care and to share with others that we are grateful.

In the past I have enjoyed helping with CLP bulk mailings, opening the mail, and more recently, other miscellaneous hand operations I can do in my own home. It is all a part of sharing the Gospel message.

Hearing responses of those who use CLP's material, blesses my innermost being and thrills me through and through.

—Sallie Brenneman

Sallie Brenneman assisted in record keeping along with receptionist duties. 1977

Improved Facilities

Looking at the two large brick buildings that house CLP's operation today, it is difficult to visualize the facilities of twenty-five years ago. Even four years ago it was different.

Just how different and just how fast those differences came about may not be as readily apparent to a new arrival as to a long-term employee. One employee remarked in 1993, "There are only three offices or work areas still at the same place they were six years ago when I came." And two of those three offices have been modified.

A visitor to CLP some time ago looked around and asked, "Was this place planned, or did it evolve?" It was an apt observation, one that can be understood only by tracing a multitude of changes, additions, adaptations, and internal rearrangements through the years.

Building No. 1, which housed all offices and production operations, until 1992. Original flat roofed building with second story added is at the left. Subsequent additions and annexations enlarged the facility to include the entire length of this building and provided an entrance on Chicago Avenue.

The office is open Monday through Friday, 8:30 a.m. to 4:30 p.m. Individuals and tour groups are welcome to visit at any time. Visitors use the street entrance or the glass entrance on the side close to the visitors' parking area.

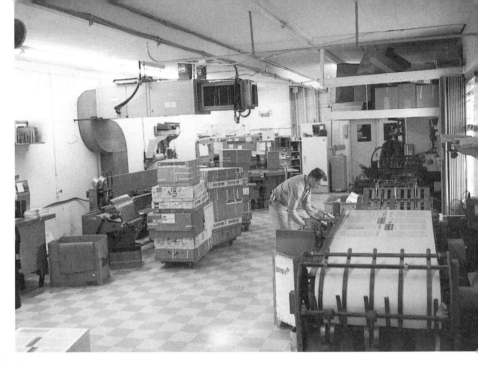

View of the old bindery in Building No. 1. Folding machines were lined up along the right side of the room; collating equipment and three-knife trimmer along the left.

Additions

In 1969 when CLP began, Sanford and Merna were renting a building from Merna's father, Aldine Brenneman, in which Aldine had operated a garage business for years. Eventually this building was deeded to the Shanks.

The original fifty-five by sixty-foot brick building has had five major additions, one of which was a second floor and one of which connected it to the aforementioned garage. The result of all these changes was one large building that looked rather oddly put together, but which did meet the needs of CLP for a number of years.

Adequate advance planning through these changes was difficult because CLP had no way of knowing how fast expansion would occur. When CLP began publishing school curriculum in 1980, however, expansion did occur. From the beginning, sales have continued to increase significantly almost every year. More sales called for more equipment, more storage area, more personnel, and thus, more space. Internal rearrangement of working areas has been common (to make an understatement). And in the accompanying clutter and confusion of moving desks, files, machines, and

131

Carol Burkholder (foreground) and Eugene Stutzman operating the Macey collator in the new pressroom built in 1979. Carol is collating by hand the first group of signatures required when a publication contains more pages than the Macey can automatically handle. (Today, one Macey has 17 stations; the other 6.)

View of the Web Pressroom, 1987 to 1992, which provided space for the two Web presses and the 17-station Macey collator. This room, which has served as the assembly room for Writer's Conference in earlier years, is also used now as the CLE Teacher Training Center.

materials, the facility has threatened more than once to burst its seams.

Internal Rearrangements

Only employees past and present would understand or find interest in the details of the many moves, but should employees from various eras of the past meet, their conversation might go something like this:

1979 employee: "I remember when the first web press was bought— at the time CLP began printing school curriculum. There was no area large enough for that press and the collating equipment purchased about the same time. So that year they built the *New Pressroom* on the back of the building, and the new equipment had a made-to-order home of its own."

1987 employee: "What you call the *New Pressroom* was *General Order Filling* area when I was there. The web presses—two of them—were lined up side by side in the center of the *Web Pressroom*, that long room in the cinder block section toward the front of the building."

1974 employee: "What you call the *Web Pressroom* was the *Mailing Room* when I was there. It had a desk for the CLP bookkeeper also and some miscellaneous bindery equipment. That was the room we cleaned out annually for Writer's Conference."

1986 employee: "That room was *Order Filling* when I was there. Bookkeeping was located in the front room next to the street. Even the street name was changed. It used to be Mt. Clinton Pike, but it became Chicago Avenue."

1994 employee: "That *New Pressroom* back in 1979 is our *Lunchroom* now. That is also where we sit down each morning for a devotional period."

1990 employee: "We had no lunchroom when I was there, and there wasn't any area with enough open space for chairs. We all stood around in the front display room for morning devotions."

1994 employee: "The web presses are now in Building No. 2—still operating side by side, but they look so much smaller and sound so much quieter since they have been moved out of what you called the *Web Pressroom*. And that *Web Pressroom* is now the *CLE Training Center*."

Such a conversation could go on indefinitely. In-house artists might talk about at least six different locations they have been. Some secretaries could name eight places their desks have been located—from one end of the building to the other, upstairs and downstairs. Proofreaders have been tucked into an uncounted number of corners on first floor, basement, second floor, and back again to first floor.

Renovation and Relocation

In the latter 80s, there was no question in anybody's mind at CLP that more room was needed. Considering the growth of the work and the continuous need to rearrange for more room for various departments, administrators gave much thought to a master plan that would revamp the entire building, and include another addition. A new outside wall could cover the irregularities created by the previous additions and affixations.

Rosalyn Strubhar receives and processes the general catalog orders and handles several hundred pieces of mail each day.

Needs in a couple of departments were acute enough that a decision was made to begin implementing certain parts of the master plan even though most of it could not be realized until more room was added.

The Computer Room, for instance, was more congested than an old-fashioned country store. The part of the building most logical for its relocation was an area on second floor occupied by the Homestudy Office, which had been moved there after outgrowing its one-room office in the basement. Furthermore, the Homestudy Office was not in a convenient location for callers, who were more and more coming directly to the CLE plant to get hands-on introduction to the curriculum.

When people came to the main office inquiring for the Homestudy Director, the receptionist would first send them back outside and show them where to enter the building at Door No.7. While they were on the way, she would notify the Homestudy Office, who would then send a personal escort to lead the callers the rest of the way.

This was far simpler than telling a stranger to go in at Door 7, go most of the way through that corner office, turn right behind the room divider, turn left and go to the top of the stairs, turn left again for a few feet, make another left turn and go the full length of the hall, turn right and go to the far end of the long front room.

Of course, the receptionist didn't actually give those directions, but neither did she say what would also have been true: "That's where the office is, but there isn't much room or accommodation there for you and your five children."

When such callers were ready to leave, someone would usually escort them out again at least as far as the stairs, because many expressed their confusion: "I'd get lost in here."

Since the master plan called for the Homestudy and Computer Departments both to have permanent space in the already existing building, it was decided that somehow these moves should be made ahead of new construction. This meant completely vacating the general CLP office, plus a large adjoining storage area. Storage materials could be moved into one of CLP's rented warehouses. But it took detailed measuring and planning plus a good deal of forbearance to move the Bookkeeping and General Office personnel with all their desks and filing cabinets and boxes from the front room near the street to the front room upstairs that was already full of writer/editors, CLP resource library, and the Homestudy Office personnel with their desks and files.

Roger Berry, whose desk was situated near the door and who was being squeezed from both sides, described that move in imPRESSions:

> Friday, August 5, 1988, will long be remembered as the day Mary Catherine and Rosalyn moved to the upstairs front office.
>
> This room is now officially the room where everything is that is not somewhere else. And I mean everything! Now the floor is well covered for those who were bothered about the need for new carpet.
>
> The main purpose of the move? To prepare for remodeling out front where CLE will eventually be located. . . . And as one of the "moved ones" suggested, so we can all keep our sense of humor.
>
> The duration of the move? Nobody knows for sure. . . . If you move to one location around here for more than six months, consider it a permanent move.
>
> Now people have been calling to the upper room and asking, "Who's there?" Answer, "We all are."

That particular arrangement lasted four months, just as long as it took crews of part-time workers to change partitions, lower ceilings, and finish walls and floors. Another employee described the next move in December:

> It's been moving time. The CLE offices are now located in the new front rooms which emerged out of the former general CLP office and adjacent storage area. . . .
>
> We have new carpet upstairs in the long front room. All the offices there have been moved out and in again. And now the computer room personnel are busily relocating themselves where CLE had been. Nobody knows how much work has been involved except those who have been doing it, and none of them have counted the steps and the miles they have put in from here to there and back again. And

nobody yet knows just where everything is or where everything is going to be when it all gets settled!

This move still didn't relieve the general crowded condition of the upstairs front room. That prevailed about four years—until after the completion of Building No. 2.

Waiting

Although the Computer Department was still crowded, the Homestudy Office was now convenient for callers. There was a front room display and a comfortable waiting area. The overall effect was a morale booster showing promise of good things to come for every department.

Rented warehouses in the community remained a necessity for several years. During that time CLP's blue ton truck made many round trips, bringing in rolls of paper to keep the presses operating, taking finished inventory to storage, and bringing it back again in smaller quantities to restock the limited space where orders were filled and shipped.

Over the years many visitors who came into the building for the first time expressed surprise at the amount of work being done in such a small building. And then there was more surprise when the building turned out to have more sections, more walkways, more rooms, more cubicles than they had envisioned from the street.

From an Employee

Doris and I were in the computer room (off Shank's kitchen) working on month-end work late one night. Irene was working in the mailing room. About 11:00 or 11:30, Irene stopped by the computer room saying she was leaving. A few minutes later she came back in and told us that the bindery room door was standing open. She closed it and went on home.

A while later Doris and I decided it was time to quit for the night! I went upstairs to put some papers on Paul's desk. As I went past the door to Merna's office I thought I heard a noise in there. I thought about turning the light on to see if I could see anything, but decided not to. When I went to Paul's office,

---

I noticed that some of the doors on the metal cabinets were open, which was rather unusual. When I returned to the computer room, I realized I had forgotten my pocketbook from my locker. I started back up to get it. Before I got to the top of the steps, I saw that there was a light on in Sanford's office. Just minutes earlier it had been dark! When I got to the locker, there were some doors open that usually were not open!

When I told Doris, we decided it was time to call for Sanford. As it turned out, Sanford was in his office, but when we told him about the bindery door and the other doors open, he decided maybe it would be good to have the police come and check. He asked us to watch for the policemen, however, since he was not dressed appropriately to meet them.

The police wanted to look first where the cabinet doors were open. Soon they were going into the stripping and dark rooms. There were two policemen. I went on back in the darkroom with one of them. Doris and the other one waited in the stripping room. While they waited, Doris heard footsteps out in the hall. About that time, Sanford walked in (in robe and slippers)! The policemen finished looking upstairs and then started downstairs. As we went into what is now the lunch room, one of the police said, "Someone could hide in here for a week and we wouldn't find him!"

After checking as carefully as possible, they decided the bindery room door likely had not been latched and had been blown open by the wind. The other doors were apparently left open carelessly.

After the police left, Doris and I went home. When I walked into the living room at home, I heard my alarm clock ringing! It was time to start a new day! So I did.

In thinking back over that night, I decided there WAS someone in Merna's office as I went past—Sanford likely was going through to his office. I'm glad I didn't turn the light on!

—Mary Alice McDorman

A New Building

While the internal changing for the Homestudy and Computer Departments was being done, plans for building an addition were

Mary Alice McDorman has worked in computer-related operations since 1985.

also being discussed. After months of planning and thousands of dollars had been spent to provide drawings and plans required by the city, CLP received a disappointing notice. The present facility did not conform to new regulations and building codes. It could continue to be used, but no outside walls could be changed. Among other problems, the south wall was located exactly on the property line, and the building did not meet current building codes for four different uses— manufacturing, business, education, and residence.

Plans for the addition were immediately scrapped, and new plans were started for a second building located the required thirty feet away from the first building. This took time. Besides the details of new construction, there were negotiations for obtaining land and discussions regarding financing and ownership.

In spite of the urgent need for space, CLP did not feel justified in accruing more debt. Only through the blessing of the Lord and vision of an able constituency did the new building (Building No. 2) become a reality. Some of the money and much labor were donated. Finances needed above that were supplied by an interested brother who shares ownership in the building to the extent of his investment, the amount of which decreases each year as CLP makes monthly payments. When the amount of his investment has been paid (without interest), CLP will have full ownership. A lease-purchase agreement is also in effect for Building No. 1.

Building No. 2 under construction in 1991. Many volunteers helped in this construction, and many others contributed funds or supplied materials at discounted rates.

Volunteers

Voluntary labor has been an important part of each of CLP's major construction projects. As Building No. 2 neared completion, the following article in *Alight* expressed the sentiment at CLP:

"So Built We the Wall..."

Nehemiah attributed the success of the wall building around Jerusalem to the Lord and to the people: "We made our prayer unto God," and ". . . the people had a mind to work."

Christian Light Publications feels a kindred spirit with Nehemiah. Today our printing and shipping facility is nearing completion, first of all because the Lord has answered prayer and made it possible. Part of His provision came through the willingness of more than two hundred volunteers who have contributed many thousands of hours and some who have sent money to pay for hired help to do what their schedules did not permit them to do. . . .

On one occasion when more help was needed and all the possibilities of volunteers seemed exhausted, our coordinator phoned a contact brother in Pennsylvania who responded, "I was just here praying about this need, but I know of no one." Later in the day he called back with a different report: "One man here in our community is closing shop and bringing his entire crew tomorrow." Tomorrow began at 2 a.m. for some of that crew, but they were here ready for work before our 7 a.m. locals arrived.

Some volunteers worked on the walls and roof in very hot August weather; some did landscaping in severe November cold. Some came one day, and at least one came as many as ten different days from out of state. Several times we had thirty to fifty volunteers on the same day. Some traveled as long as four or five hours each way besides putting in a full day's work on the job. One electrician came 3,000 miles and stayed four months. . . .

We were especially grateful for Chester Heatwole, our

Entrance to Building No. 2, facing Mt. Clinton Pike. Visitors' parking and entrance, however, should be at Building No. 1.

Aerial view of CLP.
Building No. 2 at top left. Building No. 1 is the long irregular-shaped building in the center. To the right of Building 1 you can see the Layman Apartments, Layman house (CLP has used the upstairs apartment), and the brick VS house (formerly D.R. Hostetter property). The shorter long white building to the right of Building 2 is the neighbor's chicken house used by CLP for certain types of warehouse storage.

general contractor, who offered to serve at a time when we were in crucial planning stages and very much needed just such a person. His offer included the donation of those services, and the ongoing project has involved both expenses for him as well as multiplied hours for most of the days during the past year. . . .

For all of these evidences of desire to help, we thank the Lord and those who served Him on this "Jerusalem wall." Only the Lord has a complete record of the total dollars and the total hours to be compensated for out of His supply of riches. And we believe He will reward each one for willing service.

Renovation of the old pressroom in Building No. 1 to make way for the new composition, layout, stripping, and art department areas. Here Keith Crider, who has worked for CLP several summers, has time away from committee work to help in cleanup and other aspects of renovation.

Room at Last!

Moving into the new building began in the spring of 1992. CLP was grateful for the individuals and groups of volunteers who came at various times to help with the moving. They were especially grateful for the services of Abner Riehl, who moved his family from out of state and stayed four months at no cost to CLP.

Abner efficiently engineered the process of dismantling equipment, moving it from Building No. 1 to Building No. 2, reassembling it, and getting it into operation again. With efficient help and the Lord's blessing, this move was accomplished more smoothly than had been expected.

It was a tremendous satisfaction to have space for the two web presses, three sheet-fed presses of various sizes, several platemakers, paper cutters, collators, a large rotating round table for hand collating, folding machines, hardcase book binding equipment, plastic ring binding equipment, perfect binding equipment, stitchers, drills, padding equipment, storage shelves, warehouse space, order filling areas, and mailing tables and still be able to see wide clear walkways that met OSHA requirements.

143

The following information is excerpted from a special brochure prepared for Open House of the new building, August 28, 29, 1992.

Our praise and thanks are lifted to our Lord for making this new facility possible, and our sincere appreciation goes to you, our friends, for your help in the project. Many of you gave time, energy, money, prayers, and materials for the work. Now we welcome you not only to examine our building, but to see what happens within these walls.

Since moving into the new building, we are now remodeling the old one. The first steps of the publishing and printing process are carried out in the old building. They include writing, editing, art, typesetting, layout, darkroom, and general office work. In the new building you will see the steps beginning with plate making and progressing through printing, bindery operations, warehousing, order filling, and shipping.

1. PLATEMAKERS — The first machine photographically exposes metal plates, and the second one develops them. The third one automatically exposes and develops plastic plates from original typeset copy.

2. SHEET-FED PRESSES — The small press on the left is our newest press. It is a two-color press where much of the color printing is done. The large press to the right is also a two-color press, and is used primarily for printing jobs with large sheet sizes.

3. WEB PRESSES AND PAPER STORAGE — These presses begin with rolls of paper, print on a continuous "web," and cut it into sheets at the other end. They print at speeds of 15,000 — 25,000 sheets per hour, and are capable of printing on both sides of the sheet simultaneously by using the turn-over bar.

Behind you is the storage of five kinds of roll paper we commonly use. The rolls weigh 375-450 pounds each, and have up to 5 miles of paper per roll.

4. FOLDERS — At speeds from 1 a second to 5 a second, these two machines can fold paper into various shapes and sizes. The one on the right has a continuous feed which eliminates the need for stopping to reload.

5. BOOK BINDERS — The binder in the foreground is for "perfect binding" paper-back books. It applies a plastic adhesive to the spine and attaches a cover. The books must then be trimmed.

The machine in the background is used for binding hard-case books. Previously collated pages are clamped and rolled, then glued. This allows the glue to penetrate between the sheets for a stronger bond. A strip of cloth is also glued onto the spine before the covers (which were previously glued onto heavy cardboard) are put in place. The book is then put into a clamp while the glue is drying.

6. COLLATOR / BINDER — A "signature" is a sheet of printed paper containing 4-32 pages which will be folded and used in making a book or booklet. The various signatures making a booklet (including the cover)

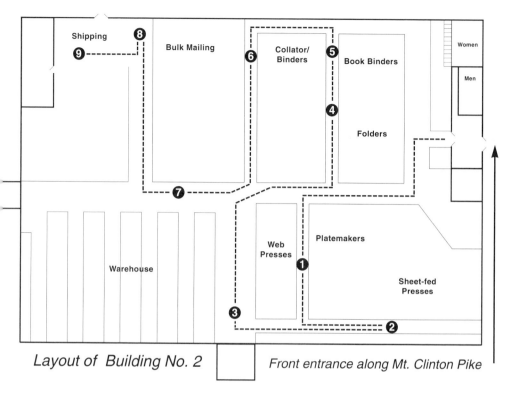

Layout of Building No. 2 | **Front entrance along Mt. Clinton Pike**

are here collated together, stapled, folded, and trimmed.

Behind you is the storage for the preprinted covers of our school curriculum LIGHTUNITs.

7. WAREHOUSE — To your left is the warehouse for the school curriculum. Beyond you on the right are the order-filling shelves. The shelves are restocked from the warehouse, and orders that have been filled from the shelves are taken to the shipping area.

8. BULK MAILING — Periodicals and bulk mailings are labeled, sorted, and bagged, ready to be distributed by the postal system. Quarterly Sunday school mailings are also done in this area. (Note the sending/receiving station for an underground tube system between the two buildings. This facilitates sending order sheets and other paperwork back and forth.)

Behind you, trade books and other general items are packaged for shipping.

9. SHIPPING — Before being shipped, orders for CLE curriculum materials that have been pulled from the shelves are compared with the original orders entered into the computer. This helps us to fill orders more accurately. The orders are then packaged and weighed, and postage is applied. We use both UPS and the postal system.

With the moving of production operations into Building No. 2, serious renovation could move ahead in Building No. 1. Some of this, too, was done by volunteers. By 1993 this renovation had provided an editorial office; a new darkroom; an enlarged computer area; more individual offices arranged in logical proximity to each other; a large carpeted area where the composition, layout, stripping, and art departments could all be in one location; a proofreading area next to composition where it is most advantageous; a lunchroom; a conference room; a library near the CLE and editorial offices; and a CLE Training Center near the CLE offices, which brought training "home" after twelve years using crowded rooms elsewhere.

The outside appearance of Building No. 1 was also improved with the addition of siding, paint, shrubbery, and a blacktop driveway and parking lot.

Has CLP moved for the last time? If the Lord delays His coming and the work continues to expand, probably not. But for now, when the CLP staff surveys the improved facilities compared with the past, they are truly thankful. They marvel at how God uses the united efforts of His people to hasten the proclamation of His truth.

A group of visitors watching the Macey collator in operation during Open House for Building No. 2 in August 1992.

Present Arrangement of Renovated Building No. 1

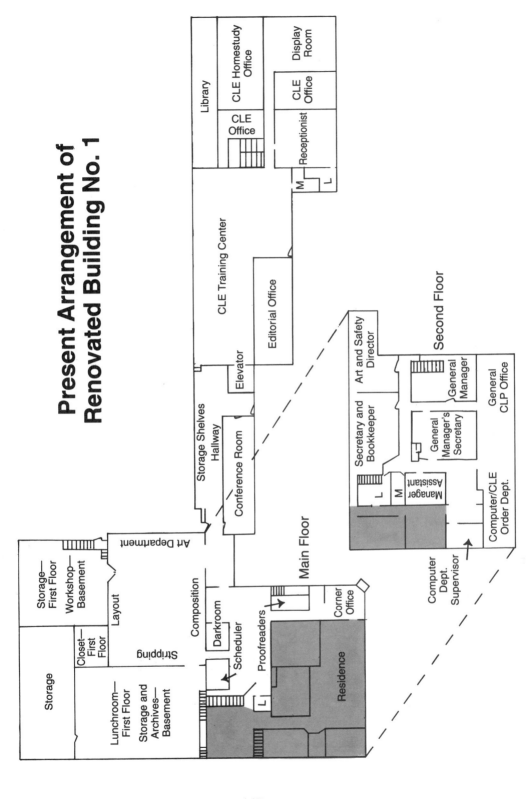

147

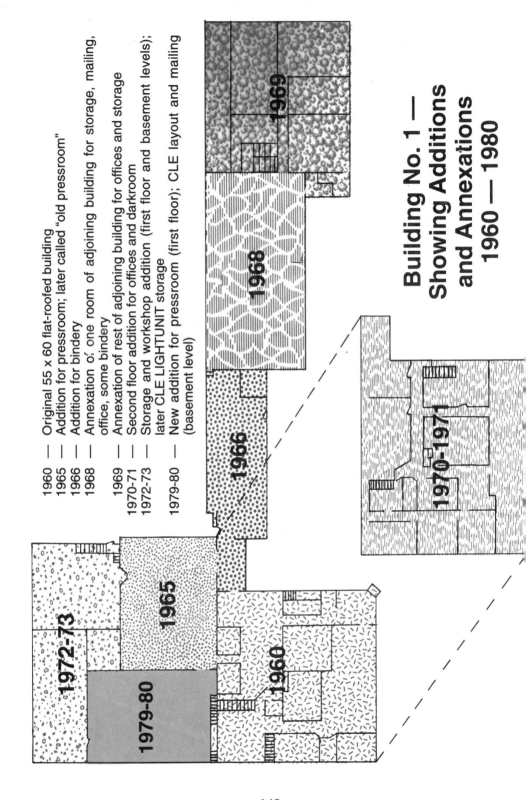

**Building No. 1 —
Showing Additions
and Annexations
1960 — 1980**

1960 — Original 55 x 60 flat-roofed building
1965 — Addition for pressroom; later called "old pressroom"
1966 — Addition for bindery
1968 — Annexation of one room of adjoining building for storage, mailing, office, some bindery
1969 — Annexation of rest of adjoining building for offices and storage
1970-71 — Second floor addition for offices and darkroom
1972-73 — Storage and workshop addition (first floor and basement levels); later CLE LIGHTUNIT storage
1979-80 — New addition for pressroom (first floor); CLE layout and mailing (basement level)

From Writer to Reader

**A short tour through the steps involved in producing a preschool quarterly—
a process which begins approximately 15 months before the date on the quarterly.**

From International Sunday School Lesson outlines, the Office Editor prepares a Preliminary Evaluation and Report, which includes suggested title, memory selection, and additional Scriptures to use if desired.

This report is then sent to a writer who prepares a guideline for the quarterly writer, including some introductory thoughts on the Scripture, lesson aims, and emphases for each lesson.

The writer's guideline is reviewed and edited by the Office Editor before it is sent to the preschool quarterly writer, who has about three months in which to complete the writing.

Lloyd Hartzler, Office Editor since 1971, prepares the Preliminary Evaluation and Report for writers; reviews and edits manuscripts.

Lula Showater handles details of scheduling all production operations.

Two copies of the manuscript are sent to the Office Editor who will immediately give one copy to the Art Director and will carefully review the other copy for content, grammar, and length.

This edited manuscript will then be given to the Scheduler to enter for production. The Scheduler prepares a detailed schedule showing the date when each step needs to be finished.

The Art Director assigns an artist to draw what is needed for the quarterly. If a search in the art files does not reveal any art on hand suitable to reuse for this particular quarter, the artist will decide what to draw and sketch rough art that will be checked by the Art Director.

Kevin Shank, the Art Director, is responsible for assigning, checking, and recording art.

Joanna Rohrer, one of the part-time staff artists, often draws quarterly art.

The artist will then produce the final art. The Art Director will receive it again for review and make a computer record, adding information about this art to the permanent file. The art is then given to the Office Editor, who will review what has been prepared and pass it on to the composition department to be placed with the typeset manuscript.

While art is being prepared, typesetting and proofreading are also being done. The typed copy is first read by a proofreading team, one reading aloud from the original manuscript and the other comparing what is read with the typed copy. Bible references are checked, and exercises are worked out to check for accuracy.

The Office Editor reviews the corrections called for and answers

Miriam Shank frequently typesets quarterly manuscripts.

Earl Martin photographs final copy, strips negatives onto flats, and makes the blueline proof copy.

questions the proofreaders may have raised. The typesetter makes needed corrections.

The corrected manuscript is then proofread the second time by a single person who reads through the copy and among other checking, verifies accuracy of all page numbers referred to in pupil or teacher materials. The typesetter corrects errors found in the second proofreading.

The manuscript is then given a final check by someone who will verify that the typist has made the corrections called for by the last proofreader.

Sterling Beachy and Steve Zimmerman at the Royal Zenith press, which is used to print large sheets of memory verse bookmarks.

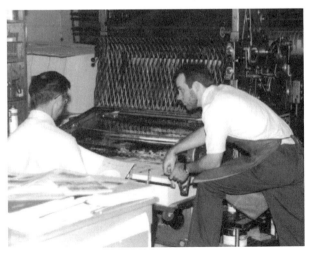

Karen Knicely operates one of the Web presses on which quarterlies are printed.

Below: Jose Liscano and Andy Korver in the bindery. This view shows both Macey collators where quarterlies are gathered, folded, and stitched.

When typesetting and art are completed, the negatives for each page are positioned on large sheets called flats. Each flat will have four quarterly pages, all held in their proper place so that finished copy will have correct margins and pages will follow each other in proper sequence. A proof copy called a blueline is made from the flats, and sheets are folded to check accuracy.

Flats are then taken to the pressroom where they are positioned on metal plates, placed under pressure in a vacuum frame, and subjected to a strong light that will burn through the negative into the light sensitive coating on the plate. Developing solution will

Crystal Shank receives Sunday school orders by mail or telephone, enters them into the computer, and sends out invoices.

Below: Julia Rhodes counting quarterlies to fill an order and placing them in the tray on the roller track; Jerry Bentz is checking orders and packing them into shipping cartons.

make the image appear on the metal plate.

The metal plate will then be put on the printing press. Ink applied to the plate will adhere only to the printed words, and this image will be transferred to a rubber blanket. Paper is printed as it passes over the rubber blanket.

Printed sheets are taken to the bindery where they are collated on the Macey, which automatically moves the book through an assembly line, adding a new sheet at each station. When the cover has been put on, the book is stitched with wire staples, then automatically folded and trimmed along the front edge. The Macey

Frieda Thiessen putting postage on a package in the mailing department. Scales and computer are tied together so that when a package is weighed, the computer screen will show the cost of different methods of shipment. The operator will choose the best option for that package, and the computer will produce a mailing label.

operator removes the finished books and places them in large metal trays ready for the order filling department.

Orders received in the mail or by telephone are entered into the computer which will produce the packing list and invoice. The packing list is sent to the order filling room where orders are accumulated in large trays and moved from one person to another on a roller track.

When all parts of the order have been assembled, the entire order is checked against the packing list and placed in a shipping carton which is taped, weighed, and labeled ready for shipping approximately 5 weeks before it will be used in Sunday school.

UPS is often the best method of shipment for Sunday school orders.

Our Daily Prayer

Over the years, CLP employees have been asked to give programs on several occasions. For one such request, the employees asked Merna Shank to write an appropriate song. Using an existing tune (written by Ray Shenk, on CLP's first Board of Directors), Merna wrote the following words, and the song was then sung by the employees.

Our Daily Prayer

Merna B. Shank

Melody R. J. Shenk; Harmony M. R. Hertzler

1. Lord, we would be a light-house tall and clear
2. Our work, O Lord, as un-to Thee we do --
3. Our dai-ly tasks are not the same for all,
4. To spread His Word of truth that all might know

Send-ing the beams of truth a-far and near.
Writ-ing and draw-ing, print-ing, mail-ing too.
But wheth-er large or mi-nor ones and small,
It lights the paths of dark-ness here be-low;

Guid-ing the seek-ing ones to fol-low Thee
The print-ed pag-es si-lent wit-ness give
These var-ied parts are need-ed all com-bined
And Lord, we pray, take all who seek for Thee

Lest they be lost and found-er in life's sea.
Yet reach the heart and tell men how to live.
To do the work our Fath-er has as-signed:
And guide them safe-ly home through life's rough sea.

Appendix A
CLP Employees

The following list includes CLP employees who were on the payroll at least six months or who have served at least one month in VS.

Some marked "VS" have received the normal VS allowance; others have provided their own board and room and served without any remuneration from CLP. Those marked "P/VS" have worked both in VS and as paid employees during their term of service.

Dates show beginning and ending times for employment, but schedules have varied. Some employees work full-time, some regular part-time, some irregular part-time, and some work at their homes. Those working for CLP from their homes as self-employed persons may not necessarily be included in this list.

Dates earlier than 1969 indicate employment by Park View Press first, with a change to the CLP payroll during the same term of service.

Besides those listed here, CLP has greatly appreciated the services of many others throughout these years who have given hours or days of voluntary service of many different kinds. Our apologies to any who should have been included but may have been missed.

Alger, Robert   (Oct. 1985 - May 1986)
   Pressroom, Bindery
Alger, Ruth (Mrs. Robert)
   (Sept. 1981 - May 1982; Nov. 1982 - Dec. 1983; Sept. 1985 - present)
   Bindery, Layout
Anderson, Ella (Mrs. Thomas)   (June 1979 - Aug. 1983)
   CLE Curriculum Development

Anderson, Susan Heatwole (Mrs. Timothy)   (Sept. 1973 - May 1993)
 Typesetting
Anderson, Thomas   (June 1979 - May 1982)
 Artist
Anderson, Timothy   (April 1980 - June 1982)
 Pressroom
Bauman, Lucinda   (Jan. 1979 - Dec. 1980; Dec. 1981 - June 1986)
 Office   P/VS
Beachy, Carol (Mrs. Ward)   (Jan. 1981 - July 1981)
 Office   VS
Beachy, Dwight R.   (Aug. 1979 - Aug. 1980)
 CLE Curriculum Development
Beachy, Sterling   (Sept. 1986 - present)
 Pressroom, Bindery, Supervisor/Management
Beachy, Ward   (Jan. 1981 - July 1981)
 Pressroom, Bindery   VS
Bechtel, Maria   (July 1986 - March 1987)
 Layout
Beery, Donna S. Ropp (Mrs. Ellis)
 (Oct. 1977 - Sept. 1983; June 1985 - April 1987)
 Typesetting
Bennett, Beadie L.   (Jan. 1979 - Feb. 1980)
 Bindery   VS
Bennett, F. Arlene   (June 1978 - Feb. 1980)
 Typesetting   P/VS
Bentz, Jerry   (Feb. 1992 - present)
 Mailing/Order-Filling, Warehouse, Supervisor/Management
Bentz, Mary Beth   (July 1993 - present)
 Mailing, Artist   P/VS
Berry, Anna Lee Barnhart (Mrs. Roger)   (Jan. 1972 - Dec. 1975)
 Office
Berry, Roger   (June 1972 - present)
 Editor, Writer, Committee
Brenneman, Betty   (Aug. 1969 - present)
 Darkroom/Stripping, Pressroom, Proofreading, Bindery
Brenneman, Sallie (Mrs. Aldine)   (1957 - present)
 Office
Brittain, Toby J. (Susie)   (May 1980 - April 1981)
 Artist, Layout
Brunk, Nancy Wile (Mrs. Harvey)   (May 1986 - Nov. 1986)
 Computer/Order Department   VS
Burkholder, Carol   (Nov. 1979 - Oct. 1982; May 1985 - July 1985)
 Bindery, Layout, Mailing/Order-Filling
Burkholder, Wesley   (June 1988 - present)
 Computer/Order Department, Supervisor/Management
Byler, Bonnie Carr (Mrs. Edward)   (Nov. 1986 - March 1988)
 Office
Byler, Susan   (Sept. 1987 - present)
 Computer/Order Department
Cash, Angela   (Aug. 1991 - present)
 Computer/Order Department

158

Coblentz, John A. (April 1979 - present)
Writer, Editor, Committee
Crider, Keith (summer 1988; summer 1989; summers 1991 - present)
Maintenance, CLE Curriculum Development, Committee
Cross, George (April 1989 - July 1990; Dec. 1990 - July 1991)
Handyman, Maintenance   VS
Cross, Verna (Mrs. George)   (April 1989 - July 1990; Dec. 1990 - July 1991)
Bindery, Office, Mailing/Order-Filling   VS
Cyzick, Douglas (Nov. 1979 - July 1982)
Mailing, Bindery, Office
Dashnaw, Martha (July 1980 - Nov. 1980)
Office, Layout   VS
Derstine, Curtis (June 1986 - June 1988)
Pressroom
Eby, Roger (Began in 1994)
Maintenance, Bindery, Pressroom   VS
Freed, Daniel (Oct. 1983 - Feb. 1984)
Office   VS
Frey, Grace (July - Aug. 1992)
Mailing/Order-Filling   VS
Friesen, Rachel (Aug. 1993 - present)
Mailing/Order-Filling   VS
Giffen, Janice Alger (Mrs. Larry)   (Sept. 1981 - May 1982)
Layout
Gingerich, Gareth (July 1980 - Nov. 1980)
Pressroom   VS
Glanzer, Eva Sonifrank (Mrs. Paul)   (June 1978 - present)
Typesetting
Gleason, Esther Leister (Mrs. James)   (Jan. 1984 - April 1984)
Bindery, Mailing   VS
Goering, James (July 1974 - Jan. 1977)
Editor
Good, Bonnie Martin (Mrs. Jonathan)
(June 1988 - Oct. 1989; May 1990 - March 1993))
Computer/Order Department, Office, Homestudy Office   P/VS
Good, Edith (July 1986 - June 1993)
Layout
Good, Kathryn Knicely (Mrs. Bruce)   (Aug. 1991 - Sept. 1993)
Bindery
Good, Kristin Hobbs (Mrs. Kelvin)   (Nov. 1984 - May 1989)
Layout, Office
Graber, Doris L. (Mrs. Alvin)   (April 1980 - March 1981)
Office
Greider, Doris (Mrs. Benjamin)   (Oct. 1976 - Aug. 1988)
Office, Computer/Order Department
Grove, Dorothy Slabaugh (Mrs. Chester)   (Aug. 1976 - April 1979)
Office
Gunick, Richard (Began in 1994)
Bindery, Pressroom, Maintenance
Harlow, Hilda (Nov. 1977 - present)
Housekeeping, Proofreading, Bindery, Mailing

Hartman, Joyce Hunsecker (Mrs. Russel)   (Dec. 1988 - June 1990)
  Mailing/Order-Filling
Hartman, Russel   (July 1987 - July 1990)
  Pressroom
Hartman, William (Bill)   (Feb. 1974 - March 1975)
  Office, Writer   VS
Hartzler, Bethany   (April 1992 - present)
  Bindery, Pressroom, Computer/Order Department, Office, Receptionist
Hartzler, David   (Summer 1992; Jan. 1994 - present)
  Mailing
Hartzler, John   (May 1971 - present)
  Pressroom, Bindery, Supervisor/Management, Committee
Hartzler, Lloyd   (May 1971 - present)
  Editor, Writer, Committee
Heatwole, Charles   (Jan. 1972 - Aug. 1975)
  Office, Committee
Heatwole, David   (Sept. 1985 - present)
  Handyman, Maintenance   VS
Heatwole, Elam   (Nov. 1989 - present)
  Maintenance, Housekeeping, Supervisor/Management, Office
Heatwole, Elizabeth (Mrs. David)   (Jan. 1979 - May 1981)
  Office   VS
Heatwole, Esther   (June 1988 - present)
  Homestudy Office
Heatwole, Fern Rohrer (Mrs. Glenn)   (Sept. 1978 - Dec. 1978)
  Office   P/VS
Heatwole, Mark   (Jan. 1978 - Dec. 1984)
  Pressroom, Bindery, Supervisor/Management
Hege, Sanford   (Nov. 1984 - Oct. 1985)
  Pressroom, Bindery   VS
Hershberger, James   (May 1992 - present)
  Homestudy Office
Hershberger, Rebecca D. Schrader (Mrs. Gary)
  (Oct. 1977 - Dec. 1978; March 1979 - Dec. 1980)
  Artist   P/VS
Hochstetler, James   (May 1980 - Aug. 1980)
  Bindery   VS
Hoff, Charles   (summer 1989; Dec. 1990 - present)
  Mailing/Order-Filling, Computer/Order Department   P/VS
Hostetter, Elizabeth   (Nov. 1981 - May 1982; Feb. 1986 - present)
  Layout, Receptionist
Jones, Dave Mickel (Mike)   (April 1979 - Oct. 1980)
  CLE Curriculum Development
Klassen, Peter   (Oct. 1981 - April 1982)
  Maintenance   VS
Klassen, Tina (Mrs. Peter)   (Oct. 1981 - April 1982)
  Housekeeping   VS
Knepp, Tabitha Coblentz (Mrs. Gary)   (May 1989 - Aug. 1989)
  Office   VS

Knicely, Beth Martin (Mrs. Blaine)
(summer 1990; June 1991 - Dec. 1991; summer 1992)
Office, Computer/Order Department, Receptionist   P/VS

Knicely, Carey   (Dec. 1991 - May 1992)
Construction/Remodeling

Knicely, Karen   (Sept. 1985 - present)
Bindery, Pressroom

Knicely, Michelle Hege (Mrs. Keith)   (Nov. 1984 - Feb. 1986)
Layout, Bindery   P/VS

Knicely, Sonia Burkholder (Mrs. Willard)   (Sept. 1992 - July 1993)
Computer/Order Department, Office, Receptionist

Korver, Andrew   (Feb. 1993 - Feb. 1994)
Pressroom, Warehouse, Bindery

Korver, Timothy   (Jan. 1981 - May 1987)
Pressroom

Kurtz, Ruby   (Aug. 1983 - July 1984)
Bindery   VS

Lahman, Grace (Mrs. Jonas)
(April 1975 - Feb. 1977; March 1977 - present at home)
Typesetting, Layout, Proofreading

Landes, Evelyn G. (Mrs. Ralph)
(Nov. 1979 - June 1980; Sept. 1980 - Feb. 1981; Sept. 1981 - Mar. 1982)
Layout, Bindery

Landis, David   (Sept. 1985 - April 1987)
Pressroom, Mailing/Order-Filling

Layman, Jane   (June 1981 - Dec. 1990)
Office, Homestudy Office

Layman, Treda   (Sept. 1992 - present)
Artist

Liscano, Jose   (March 1990 - present)
Bindery, Spanish Translation

Long, Ronald   (Oct. 1982 - Feb. 1985)
Bindery

Lowry, James   (Aug. 1973 - Oct. 1979)
Writer

Martin, Curvin   (Nov. 1989 - Aug. 1991)
Construction/Remodeling, Typesetting, Pressroom   P/VS

Martin, Earl   (April 1989 - present)
Pressroom, Darkroom/Stripping

Martin, Edna Ruth Yoder (Mrs. Harold)   (June 1980 - Aug. 1980)
Layout   VS

Martin, Jean Hartman (Mrs. Curvin)   (Feb. 1986 - Aug. 1991)
Bindery, Darkroom   P/VS

Martin, John D.
(Aug. 1971 - Aug. 1973; June 1974 - Sept. 1974; Oct. 1975 - March 1976)
Writer

Martin, Kim Glenn (Mrs. Vernon)   (June 1979 - Dec. 1979)
Artist, Darkroom/Stripping

Martin, Marlene Heatwole (Mrs. David)   (May 1981 - Jan. 1984)
Computer/Order Department, Office

Proclaiming God's Truth

Martin, Mary   (April 1987 - Dec. 1992)
Bindery, Pressroom   P/VS
Martin, Miriam E.   (April 1992 - April 1993; on call presently)
Bindery
Martin, Miriam I.   (June 1979 - April 1988)
Artist
Martin, Patricia Shank (Mrs. John D.)   (April 1976 - April 1979)
Office
Martin, Rosalie   (April 1989 - Nov. 1992)
Office, Darkroom, Layout   P/VS
Martin, Ruth K.   (June 1980 - June 1981; Sept. 1983 - April 1988)
Layout, Office
Martin, Shirley A. Horst (Mrs. Dean)   (Jan. 1980 - Dec. 1980)
Mailing/Order-Filling, Layout   VS
Martin, Verna Sensenig (Mrs. John H.)   (June 1974 - Dec. 1974)
Artist, Layout   VS
Martin, Willodean   (Oct. 1982 - Oct. 1983)
Office, Mailing/Order-Filling   VS
Mast, Cynthia A. Bennett (Mrs. Paul)   (Jan. 1978 - Dec. 1978)
Typesetting   P/VS
McDorman, Mary Alice   (Sept. 1985 - present)
Computer/Order Department, Office
Miller, Darlene   (July - Aug. 1993)
Mailing/Order-Filling   VS
Miller, David W.   (Aug. 1988 - present)
Office, Artist
Miller, Fred W.   (July 1981 - present)
Committee, Writer, Editor, Director of CLE Training and Field Services
Miller, Joseph   (April 1986 - Sept. 1986)
Bindery   VS
Miller, Lula A.   (June 1979 - Aug. 1979)
Layout   VS
Myers, Naomi (Mrs. Wilmer)   (Sept. 1985 - present)
Bindery, Pressroom, Proofreading
Nisly, Gerald W.   (Dec. 1980 - April 1981)
Handyman   VS
Nisly, Mary Ruth   (July 1979)
Layout   VS
Nisly, T. Millard   (Oct. 1978 - March 1979)
Pressroom, Construction/Remodeling   VS
Nolt, Bonnie Horst (Mrs. Kenneth)   (Oct. 1980 - Dec. 1980)
Bindery   VS
Pawling, James W.   (Sept. 1980 - July 1983)
Computer/Order Department
Pence, Loretta Martin (Mrs. David)   (April 1985 - April 1986)
Layout   VS
Peters, Peter
(Aug. 1983 - present; Aug. 1983 - July 1984 on premises; continues from home)
CLE Curriculum Development, Writer   P/VS
Plank, Donna   (March 1987 - present)
Mailing/Order-Filling, Bindery

Putnam, Charlotte L. Martin (Mrs. Cal) (Feb. 1975 - Dec. 1975)
Office   VS

Ramer, Judith E. Lehman (Mrs. Seth) (Sept. 1979 - Feb. 1981)
Layout

Ray, Derrick (Aug. 1983 - April 1984)
Bindery

Reed, Ethel (Mrs. Paul) (May 1985 - present)
Homestudy Office

Reed, Paul (July 1979 - present)
Homestudy Office, Supervisor/Management

Reimer, Gerry (Nov. 1989 - Nov. 1990)
Construction/Remodeling, Pressroom   VS

Reimer, Myrna (Mrs. Gerry) (Nov. 1989 - Nov. 1990)
Office   VS

Rhodes, Julia (Sept. 1991 - present)
Bindery, Computer/Order Department, Office, Receptionist

Rhodes, Mary Nell (Feb. 1984 - present)
Proofreading

Rhodes, Nancy S. Rhodes (Mrs. Robert) (Aug. 1977 - April 1978)
Office

Risser, Bonita (May 1984 - Dec. 1987)
Bindery, Pressroom

Risser, John D. (Jan. 1972 - Dec. 1982; irregular basis 1983 - 1984)
Committee

Roberg, Robert (Sept. 1984 - Aug. 1985)
Bindery   VS

Rohrer, Catherine Christner (Mrs. Linden)
(May 1976 - Aug. 1977; Feb. 1978 - May 1979)
Office

Rohrer, James (June 1979 - July 1983)
Bindery, Art Coordinator, Office   P/VS

Rohrer, Joanna (Sept. 1990 - present)
Artist

Rohrer, Wilma
(Jan. 1980 - Dec. 1981; June 1982 - June 1984; March 1985 - Dec. 1987;
summer 1989; summer 1990; Oct. 1992 - present)
Layout, Office, Computer/Order Department, Typesetting

Schrock, Faith (Jan. 1980 - Feb. 1980)
Layout   VS

Schrock, Loveda Hochstetler (Mrs. Wendell) (July 1978 - Aug. 1978)
Artist   VS

Schrock, Lucinda Heatwole (Mrs. Allen) (July 1973 - April 1976)
Office, Receptionist

Schrock, Titus (April 1973 - March 1975)
Bindery   P/VS

Schwartz, Abraham (Aug. 1979 - Sept. 1981)
CLE Curriculum Development, Committee

Schwartz, Carol (Mrs. Wayne) (Jan. 1988 - Dec. 1988)
Computer/Order Department   VS

Schwartz, Wayne (Jan. 1988 - Dec. 1988)
Maintenance, Construction/Remodeling   VS

Shank, Carol   (Oct. 1974 - present)
   Office, Art Coordinator, Permissions Secretary   P/VS
Shank, Crystal   (Jan. 1979 Aug. 1989; Aug. 1990 - present)
   Bookkeeper, Computer/Order Department, Editor, Office   P/VS
Shank, Esther (Mrs. Rawley)   (Dec. 1988 - Feb. 1991)
   Typesetting
Shank, James T.   (May 1993 - present)
   Bindery, Housekeeping, Mailing/Order-Filling   VS
Shank, Kevin D.   (Jan. 1985 - present)
   Pressroom, Art Department, Supervisor/Management
Shank, Merna (Mrs. Sanford)   (1957 - present)
   Office, Secretary of the Board, Proofreading, Editor, Writer, Committee   P/VS
Shank, Miriam Breneman   (Mrs. Sterling)
   (Oct. 1979 - Aug. 1980; Sept. 1982 - present)
   CLE Curriculum Development, Typesetting, Editor   P/VS
Shank, Sanford L.   (1957 - 1990)
   President, Committee, Supervisor/Management, CLE Curriculum Development
   P/VS
Shank, Sterling   (Jan. 1984 - April 1991)
   Pressroom, CLE Curriculum Development, Typesetting, Office   P/VS
Sheffield, Samuel C.   (Dec. 1978 - Feb. 1979)
   Bindery   VS
Shenk, Zela   (Jan. 1967 - present)
   Mailing/Order-Filling, Office, Bindery, Proofreading   P/VS
Shoemaker, Catherine (Mrs. Matthew)   (June 1981 - Nov. 1982)
   Mailing/Order-Filling, Bindery
Shoemaker, Matthew   (Oct. 1977 - Jan. 1987)
   Mailing, CLE Curriculum Development   P/VS
Showalter, Hettie E.   (Nov. 1979 - Aug. 1980)
   Layout   P/VS
Showalter, Lula   (Aug. 1976 - present)
   Bindery, Pressroom, Receptionist, Office, Layout
Showalter, Mary Catherine   (Dec. 1969 - Sept. 1992; Dec. 1993 - present)
   Bookkeeper, Office   P/VS
Showalter, Sarah Showalter (Mrs. Michael)
   (Sept. 1979 - Feb. 1980; Aug. 1980 - Dec. 1980)
   Mailing/Order-Filling, Layout, Bindery
Solberg, Elinor Hofer (Mrs. Jeff)   (Jan. 1984 - May 1984)
   Office   VS
Sommers, Eugene   (Nov. 1975 - May 1976)
   Artist
Stauffer, Irene   (July 1984 - April 1990)
   Mailing/Order-Filling   P/VS
Stoltzfus, Mary Louise   (Dec. 1979 - Aug. 1981)
   CLE Curriculum Development
Strite, Rhonda Hobbs (Mrs. Kent)   (June 1986 - June 1990)
   Layout
Strubhar, Christine Schrock (Mrs. Joseph)
   (June 1979 - Feb. 1980; May 1980 - March 1981)
   Artist, Layout   VS
Strubhar, Joseph H.   (Jan. 1979 - March 1981)
   Pressroom   P/VS

Strubhar, Mary   (Oct. 1989 - Nov. 1990)
Office   VS
Strubhar, Rosalyn (Mrs. Roy)   (Jan. 1987 - present)
Office
Strubhar, Roy   (Jan. 1987 - present)
Mailing/Order-Filling
Strubhar, Susie   (Aug. - Nov. 1991)
Bindery, VS House Hostess   VS
Strubhar, Willie   (Aug. - Nov. 1991)
Handyman, Construction/Electrician   VS
Stutzman, Alice J. Reber (Mrs. Eugene)   ((June 1980 - Aug. 1981)
Office, Bindery   P/VS
Stutzman, Eugene D.   (March 1980 - May 1982)
Bindery   P/VS
Swartz, John R.   (June 1979 - present)
CLE Curriculum Development, Committee
Thiessen, Edna (Mrs. John)   (Aug. 1992 - May 1993)
Bindery, Mailing/Order-Filling   VS
Thiessen, Frieda
(July 1990 - Dec. 1990; Feb. 1991 - Oct. 1991; July 1992 - Jan. 1994)
Mailing/Order-Filling   VS
Thiessen, John   (Aug. 1992 - May 1993)
Maintenance, Construction/Remodeling   VS
Thiessen, Melvin   (Aug. 1992 - April 1993)
Maintenance, Construction/Remodeling   VS
Tice, Orpha   (June 1979 - Aug. 1981)
CLE Curriculum Development   VS
Weaver, Jeffrey   (March 1988 - March 1989)
Pressroom   VS
Weber, Mary Gingerich (Mrs. Kenneth)   (June 1976 - Feb. 1978)
Layout, Typesetting, Office   P/VS
Wenger, Ray M.   (June 1974 - March 1976)
Writer
Wenger, Rhoda (Mrs. Ray)   (June 1974 - May 1975)
Office
Wilkins, Chevie   (March 1985 - Dec. 1985)
Layout   P/VS
Wilkins, Una Lee (Mrs. Grant)   (Feb. 1979 - May 1982)
Layout, Proofreading, Bindery
Wilson, Robert   (April 1990 - present)
Mailing/Order Filling, CLE Curriculum Development, Office, Committee
Witmer, Ernest   (May 1986 - Feb 1987; irregular basis following 1987)
Writer
Witmer, Rachel Schrader (Mrs. Ernest)   (June 1980 - Aug. 1980)
Layout   VS
Witmer, Ruby   (Nov. 1975 - May 1976)
Office   VS
Yoder, Andrew H.   (May 1976 - Oct. 1977; May 1980 - March 1981)
Artist
Yoder, Elmina   (June 1979 - Aug. 1979; May 1980 - June 1980)
Layout   VS

Yoder, Lois Bontrager (Mrs. Ed)   (Oct. 1981 - April 1982)
Office   VS
Yoder, M. Mark   (July 1985 - June 1986)
Bindery, Maintenance
Yoder, Mark   (Dec. 1983 - March 1984)
Writer
Yoder, Millard   (Dec. 1980 - March 1981)
Bindery   VS
Yoder, Norman   (Aug. 1991 - present)
Typesetting, Supervisor/Management   P/VS
Yoder, Phyllis A. Hochstetler (Mrs. Arlan)   (Nov. 1977 - March 1978)
Office   VS
Yoder, Ruthanna Schrader (Mrs. Mark)   (Aug. 1980 - Sept. 1980)
Layout   VS
Zimmerman, Miriam Yoder (Mrs. Gerald)   (Nov. 1988 - Dec. 1989)
Computer/Order Department
Zimmerman, Stephen   (March 1992 - April 1994)
Warehouse, Pressman

Some local VSers who have regularly been on call or who have given many hours of service without remuneration, but are not necessarily listed as employees:

Paul and Vivian Benner
Anna Brubaker
James Brubaker
Mary Brubaker
Mary Deputy Brubaker
Vada Brunk
Harold and Bertha Campbell
Vernon and Hazel Good
Alma Hartzler
Earl and Eunice Hartzler
Ruby Hartzler
David and Elizabeth Heatwole
Margaret Shank

The following employees were much involved with CLP work and personnel, but were only on the Park View Press payroll during their employment.

Anderson, Stephen   (June 1979 - Dec. 1980)
Barnhart, Coleen Heatwole (Mrs. Glen)   (Sept. 1969 - Dec. 1972)

Barnhart, Hilda Swartz (Mrs. Philip)   (Sept. 1971 - Nov. 1975)
Basinger, David W.   (Feb. 1971 - Feb. 1981)
Beery, Lydia Ann   (Sept. 1965 - Jan. 1981)
Brenneman, Aldine   (1957 - Dec. 1985)
Brubaker, Harold   (Sept. 1963 - Feb. 1978)
Brubaker, Mary   (Nov. 1965 - June 1981)
Burkholder, David L.   (June 1962 - Dec. 1977)
Burkholder, Marion   (Sept. 1968 - Mar. 1973)
Campbell, Catherine Good (Mrs. John Paul)   (June 1974 - March 1977)
Campbell, Eldwin   (Aug. 1968 - Nov. 1969; June 1970 - Sept. 1977)
Campbell, Vera Rose Heatwole (Mrs. Eldwin)   (May 1969 - May 1972)
Custer, Ann   (Oct. 1969 - July 1986)
Faggella, Goldie (Mrs. Frank)   (Apr. 1963 - Oct. 1973)
Good, Anna Slabaugh (Mrs. Darrell)   (June 1976 - June 1978)
Good, Edwin   (June 1967 - June 1971)
Good, Hazel (Mrs. Vernon)   (Oct. 1969 - Mar. 1973; Mar. 1976 - Oct. 1976)
Graber, Julia Heatwole (Mrs. Paul)
        (June - Aug. 1970; June 1971 - May 1973; summer 1976)
Hartzler, Ruby (Mrs. John)   (Aug. 1971 - Apr. 1973)
Heatwole, Arline Campbell (Mrs. Mark)   (Mar. 1972 - Feb. 1980)
Heatwole, Naomi Hartzler (Mrs. Wendell)   (Nov. 1972 - Aug. 1974)
Horst, Dale   (Oct. 1980 - Mar. 1981)
Horst, Kenneth   (June 1970 - Dec. 1972)
Horst, Mahlon   (Feb. 1969 - June 1975)
Idlewine, William (Bill)   (Jan. 1975 - Nov. 1976)
Kulp, Nona Sonifrank (Mrs. Roger)   (Nov. 1969 - Oct. 1975)
Landis, Esther Martin (Mrs. John)   (Apr. 1973 - Oct. 1973)
Mallow, Mary Grace Lahman (Mrs. Larry)   (Sept. 1974 - Aug. 1977)
Martin, Merle E.   (Jan. 1966 - Dec. 1971)
Martin, Mildred (Mrs. Merle)   (Aug. 1964 - July 1976)
Mast, Paul D.   (Nov. 1976 - Feb. 1977; Nov. 1977 - Apr. 1978; June 1978 - Nov. 1978)
Moore, Bonnie Good (Mrs. Jim)   (Feb. 1973 - Oct. 1973)
Myers, Bonita Eshleman (Mrs. Tim)   (Aug. 1974 - Oct. 1975)
O'Brien, Margaret Smith (Mrs. Michael)   (Apr. 1969 - July 1970)
Petre, Daniel   (Aug. 1977 - Apr. 1978)
Petre, Lawrence   (Oct. 1976 - Nov. 1981)
Petre, Norma (Mrs. Lawrence)   (June 1978 - Dec. 1981)
Shank, Boyd L.   (1957 - Oct. 1971; Oct. 1972 - Oct. 1980)
Shank, Peggy   (July 1977 - Dec. 1981)
Shank, Richard E.   (May 1980 - Apr. 1981)
Showalter, Anna V.   (Sept. 1980 - May 1983)
Showalter, Ethel Showalter (Mrs. Kenneth)   (Aug. 1969 - Sept. 1971)
Showalter, Stella Rhodes (Mrs. Steven)   (Sept. 1973 - Apr. 1976)
Snyder, John M.   (Feb. 1969 - Jan. 1973)
Stoltzfus, Carolyn Good (Mrs. Clifford)   (Aug. 1977 - Jan. 1979)
Swartz, Carroll, Jr.   (Dec. 1972 - June 1973)

Syharath, Keovilay   (Aug. 1980 - Mar. 1981)
Trissel, Iva   (Jan. 1970 - Dec. 1981)
Turner, Mylinda Howard (Mrs. Cletus)   (Sept. 1979 - July 1981)
Weber, Leonard   (Feb. 1977 - Mar. 1978)
Witmer, Edith Martin (Mrs. Eldon)   (Apr. 1973 - Sept. 1973)
Yoder, Martha Hostedler (Mrs. Leon)   (Sept. 1970 - June 1971)

Appendix B
Directors / Advisors / Editors

* indicates present position

Board of Directors

Sanford L. Shank, Chairman 1969-1990
Merna B. Shank, 1969-1972
Ray J. Shenk, 1969-1982, Emeritus 1982-1985
Enos Heatwole, 1970-1981
*** Lloyd Hartzler**, 1970 to the present
Charles Heatwole, 1972-1978
Glen Good, 1976-1981
Lester Heatwole, 1978-1981
*** Glenn Martin**, 1979 to the present
Paul Reed, 1979-1988
Ben Greider, 1980-1992
*** Richard Shank**, 1982 to the present; President since 1990
Glenn Schrock, 1988-1990
*** Leon Yoder**, 1988 to the present; Chairman beginning 1990
*** John Hartzle**r, 1990 to the present
*** Mark Heatwole**, Associate 1990; 1991 to the present
*** David G. Martin**, Associate 1994

Advisors

*** Ervin Hershberger**, 1973 to the present
Lloyd Kropf, 1973-1993
Leighton Martin, 1973-1986
George Reed, 1973-1988
*** Harry Schrock**, 1973 to the present

    * **David Showalter**, 1973 to the present
    Paul Smith, 1973-1989
    Irvin Shank, 1975-1990
    David Stutzman, 1977-1985
    Glenn Martin, 1979 (became Board Member)
    Fred Miller, 1980-1982 (became employee)
    * **Gerald Eshleman**, 1982 to the present
    * **Wilford Stutzman**, 1983 to the present
    James Roth, 1985-1989
    Olen Miller, 1985-1990
    * **Howard Bean**, 1986 to the present
    * **Caleb Stauffer**, 1989 to the present
    * **John Brunk**, 1989 to the present
    * **Gerald Kilmer**, 1990 to the present
    * **Ray Shaum**, 1990 to the present
    * **Glenn Schrock**, 1991 to the present

Editors

Book and Tract Committee
    * **John Coblentz**, 1981 to the present

CLP Office Editor
    * **Lloyd Hartzler**, 1971 to the present

Alight
    Sanford and Merna Shank, 1987-1990
    * **Merna Shank**, 1991 to the present

CLE LightLines
    * **Paul E. Reed**, 1980 to the present

Companions
    David L. Burkholder, 1973-1983
    * **Roger L. Berry**, 1983 to the present
        "Truth for Youth" column
        * **Roger Berry**, 1973 to the present
        "Science and the Scriptures" column
        * **Paul Reed**, 1973 to the present
        "Archaeology and the Scriptures" column
        * **Roger Berry**, 1973 to the present
        "Program Projector" column
            John D. Risser, 1973-1983
            Ross Ulrich, 1984-1986
            Eli W. Martin, 1986-1994
        * **Ronald Henry**, began in 1994

Partners / Story Mates
    Evelyn Brunk Bear, 1972-1976
    Mildred L. Martin, Co-editor 1977-1989
    Rose Trissel, Co-editor 1977-1980

Ellen Heatwole, Co-editor, 1980-1982
Crystal R. Shank, Co-editor, 1982-1989

Partners
 ***Crystal R. Shank**, 1989 to the present

Story Mates
 ***Miriam R. Shank**, 1989 to the present

Appendix C
CLP Publications

The following dates indicate the year CLP copyrighted an item, obtained rights to publish, or first printed their own edition of another publisher's work.

1970

The Broken Hedge (tract)
John Wesley Distressed! Charles G. Finney Confesses! (tract)
Just for You — first issue
Personal Work
Personal Work Memory Cards
Questionable Statements Regarding the Atonement
The Teacher's Friend
Who Are the Mennonites? (tract)

1971

Allegheny Gospel Trails
Assorted Christian school brochures
Berean VIII Bible Achievement Test
Christopher Dock, Pioneer Christian Schoolmaster on the Skippack
Christopher Dock Picture
Our Wedding Day Prayer (card)
Paul's Letter to the Corinthians
A Teacher's Pledge (card)
Walking in the Spirit (card)
"When Jesus Comes" Motto

1972

Arrive Alive
Berean VI Bible Achievement Test
Personal Appearance in the Light of God's Word
Sunday School Curriculum; Story Mates and Partners

1973

Calvinism—Arminianism, Which? (tract)
Christian Literature Supplement
Companions — first issue
Creative Touch I
Cry of the Northland
For His Sake
Who's Got Your Tongue? (tract)

1974

Godward or Worldward—Which? (tract)
Living Together on God's Earth
A Morning Prayer (song sheet)
Pilgrim's Progress Study Guides, Part I and Part II
Under God's Arrest
Why I Couldn't Fight

1975

Apariencia Personal en la Luz de la Palabra de Dios
Practical Pointers for Training Your Child
The Story of God's People
You and Your Bible / You and Your Life

1976

Answering the Cry
The Christian and Romans 7
Calvinismo—Arminianismo, ¿Cual? (tract)
The Eternal Security Teaching
Eternity (tract)
God's World—His Story
Green Lights Phonics

1977

Beyond Death
Bookmarks: Strength in Silence and Prayer of Serenity
Five Little Andys
Handbook for Christian Writers
Happy Life Stories
Note Cards: Mountain Scene; Flower Garden
Why I Am a Conscientious Objector (tract)

1978

Camp of Israel Map
Ozark Parson
Summer Bible School Curriculum

1979

The Doctrine of Nonresistance (Study Guide)
FBI Challenges Conscientious Objector
Note Cards: Squirrel Design
Story Time With Grandma

1980

CLE Curriculum
North America Is the Lord's
Praises We Sing

1981

Bible Teaching on Divorce and Remarriage
A Call to Creative Protest (tract)
I Corinthians—Epistle of Correction and Exhortation (Study Guide)
In the Whale's Belly
Little Ones Praise
Shadow of Death
The Significance of the Christian Woman's Veiling
Whedon's Commentary: Matthew/Mark; Luke/John

1982

Creative Touch II
God's Marvelous Gifts
The Gospel of John (Study Guide)

Los Menonitas—¿Quienes Son? ¿Que Creen? (tract)
Nonresistance Study
Perspectives of Truth in Literature
The Unfolding Plan of Redemption
What the Bible Says About Child Training (Study Guide)

1983

The Attributes of God (Study Guide)
But Not Forsaken
Dilek
Hidden Riches
Making Melody #1
Mode of Baptism (tract)
No Sipping Saints, Please (tract)
Simple Life Coloring Book

1984

Journal of Tears
Making Melody #2
Redemption Revealed (Study Guide)

1985

Making Melody #3
Nonresistance or Pacifism—Which? (tract)
True Discipleship (Study Guide)
Unto the Hills

1986

At Every Gate a Pearl
Ewigkeit
From Wealth to Faith
Making Melody #4
Martyr of the Catacombs
Music in Biblical Perspective
Music in Biblical Perspective (Study Guide)
Nonconformity Study

1987

"Alight" — first issue

Glimpses of Mennonite History and Doctrine (Study Guide)
Making Melody #5
Tangle With Fear

1988

Bible Studies for New Believers
Circle of Love
Creative Touch III
The Errors of Calvinism vs. the Biblical View of God and Man
   (Study Guide)
Making Melody #6
Ordination Certificates

1989

Assurance of Salvation
Assurance of Salvation (Study Guide)
The Bible Mode of Baptism
Harvest of Tears
Math at Work
Mennoniten—Wer Sind Sie? Was Glaben Sie?

1990

Are Written Standards for the Church?
Hannah Is a Helper
Heaven at Last
Making Melody #7
One-Anothering (Study Guide)
Tea Leaves

1991

Belize—Land by the Carib Sea
I and II Peter (Study Guide)
God Made Them All
Happy Ways
Into All the World
My Soul's Delights
Nature Study of Belize
Stories I like to Read
Thankful Days

1992

Adventures on Lilac Hill
Awaiting the Dawn
Christian Family Living
  Courtship That Glorifies God
  God's Will for Love in Marriage
  God's Will for My Body
  Singlehood That Glorifies God
  What the Bible Says About Marriage, Divorce, and Remarriage
Christian Family Living, Part I (Study Guide)
Estudios Biblicas Para Nuevos Creyentes
For One Moment
Little Ones Praise Tape
Lucy Winchester
Palace Beautiful
Rights to publish former Herald Press tracts
  (some new titles produced)
A Tree Is Special
The Victorious Life

1993

Answers to Anxiety
Assorted tracts
Called to Be a Layman
Christian Family Living, Part II (Study Guide)
The Christian and the State
What the Bible Says About Child Training

1994

Assorted tracts
The Victorious Life (Study Guide)
Markie and the Hammond Cousins
Little Church House by the River
Proclaiming God's Truth

Christian Light Publications, Inc., is a nonprofit conservative Mennonite publishing company providing Christ-centered, Biblical literature in a variety of forms including Gospel tracts, books, Sunday school materials, summer Bible school materials, and a full curriculum for Christian day schools and homeschools.

For more infomation at no obligation or for spiritual help, please write to us at:

Christian Light Publications, Inc.
P. O. Box 1212
Harrisonburg, VA 22801-1212